# Overruled

# Overruled

## Confronting Our Vanishing Democracy in 8 Cases

### SAM FOWLES

A Oneworld Book

As of the time of initial publication, the URLs displayed in this book link or refer to existing websites on the Internet. Oneworld Publications Ltd is not responsible for, and should not be deemed to endorse or recommend, any website other than its own or any content available on the Internet (including without limitation at any website, blog page, information page) that is not created by Oneworld Publications Ltd.

First published in Great Britain, the Republic of Ireland and Australia by Oneworld Publications, 2022
The paperback edition published 2023

ISBN 978-0-86154-532-2
eISBN 978-0-86154-248-2

Typeset by Hewer Text UK Ltd, Edinburgh
Printed and bound in Great Britain by Clays Ltd, Elcograf S.p.A.

Oneworld Publications
10 Bloomsbury Street
London WC1B 3SR
England

Stay up to date with the latest books,
special offers, and exclusive content from
Oneworld with our newsletter

Sign up on our website
**oneworld-publications.com**

For my parents (who taught me how to be a person),
Ryan, Estelle and Clare (who taught me how to be
a barrister) and Vicki (who's just the best).

# CONTENTS

# FOREWORD: CAN TIKTOK SAVE DEMOCRACY?

Since *Overruled* was published, the parlous state of our democratic constitution has been laid bare. Decisions that affect every part of our lives have been made, imposed and overturned, with none of us having a say in it. When I speak about saving our endangered democracy, I get asked the same question: is there any cause for hope? I give the same answer every time: TikTok. It's not the platform itself that inspires me – it's the users. Young people (Generation Z and Millennials) have received nothing but scorn from those in power. We're derided as 'snowflakes' while our chances for secure jobs, long-term savings, homes and a safe climate are determinedly obliterated. Yet we are sharing ideas and organising – from 'digital Pride' in 2020 to the school climate strikes and Black Lives Matter. Many young people report researching a company's ethics before buying its products.

Movements led by these younger generations have shown us that democracy is not simply a legislative system: it survives and flourishes through the efforts and belief of citizens. In September 2022, along with a group of other lawyers, academics and parliamentarians, I founded the Institute for Constitutional and

Democratic Research, bringing together leading thinkers to defend the idea of democracy – and spread it widely. We all know that politics isn't working. The ICDR aims to empower citizens to find real solutions – starting first and foremost with rebuilding democratic values.

When *Overruled* came out, I warned that we faced a choice about whether we wanted to live in a democracy at all. Since then, the choice has only gotten starker. When the book was published, I was instructed in a parliamentary inquiry into judicial independence. We concluded that the government's repeated attacks on judges breached constitutional norms. In 2022 the UK saw three different Prime Ministers. Not one had a genuine popular majority. Boris Johnson won the 2019 election because the gerrymandered British electoral system gave him an overwhelming parliamentary majority, despite getting just 46% of the popular vote. Johnson wound down his premiership by appointing a series of political allies, donors and flunkies to the House of Lords, aptly highlighting the absurdity of a democracy in which so much of the legislature is hand-picked by the executive.

Johnson was followed by Liz Truss. She took the reins in an election from which 99% of the population were excluded. After crashing the economy in her first month, she was forced out of office, not by voters (who had no choice about her premiership or her successor), but by the City and party powerbrokers. Then came Rishi Sunak, who became PM without so much as a contest within the Conservative Party. He immediately jettisoned his predecessors' manifesto commitments, imposing a programme on which voters never had a say. The multiple economic and social crises wracking the nation flow from the lack of accountability in our government. A shadowy group of lobbyists and donors concocted Truss's disastrous 'mini-budget'.

The views of this coterie were prioritised over the interests of citizens – and their influence was shielded from public scrutiny. This is increasingly just how our system works: an ICDR report in August 2022 revealed that MPs and ministers have greater structural incentives to address the needs of donors than voters. The 2022 crash was the year's most dramatic example of the perverse incentives which infect our politics, but it was by no means the only one.

Citizens are systematically disempowered. Under new legislation, any protest deemed too disruptive by police or ministers can be banned. The death of Elizabeth II provided a pretext to crack down on opposition to the monarchy. Ministers now demand that schools and universities provide only favourable coverage of Britain's imperial past. The politicisation of public institutions continues apace. In May 2022 Durham Police, at the instigation of the government and its supporters, reopened an investigation into an alleged breach of lockdown regulations by the Leader of the Opposition, having already concluded that no crime had been committed. Meanwhile the Metropolitan Police refused to investigate allegations that members of the executive committed the same offences until their hand was forced by a judicial review.

The concentration of power in the hands of private individuals or organisations is just as damaging to democracy as the concentration of power in the hands of the government. The impacts of this are writ large by billionaire Elon Musk's takeover of Twitter. Within weeks one of the world's largest social media platforms was recalibrated to privilege the hard-right views adopted by its new owner. This further distorts the prism through which many voters see the world, closes down spaces for dissenting ideas and increases the risk of harassment and violence for the minoritised.

But it's too early to despair. Our democracy has been fortunate in its adversaries. Putative autocrats chase power with ruthless efficiency, but they can be remarkably ineffective once in control. By the end of 2022, the UK's executive made itself so unpopular that, despite the many measures that governments have taken to ensure that they cannot lose power (many of which are detailed in this book!), it may lose the next election. This is by no means a given. 2023 began with government moves to use new voter ID laws to exclude Gen Z and Millennials from voting (by favouring ID not available to young people) and ramping up its culture war with attacks on immigrants and trans people. We will likely see further assaults on democratic rights and an all-out push to convince the nation to blame invented enemies, and not those in power, for its woes.

If, however, opposition parties can find a way to prevail, the next decade presents an historic opportunity for democratic reform. Citizens, led by Millennials and Gen Z, are seizing the mantle and calling for our government to be accountable to us. We must grasp the moment to turn the ship of state around and reorient towards the democratic lodestar of the constitution.

St Edmund Hall
University of Oxford
December 2022

# INTRODUCTION

*. . . the failures of investigation and disclosure were in our judgment so egregious as to make the prosecution of any of the 'Horizon cases' an affront to the conscience of the court.*

Holroyde LJ, Hamilton and Ors v Post
Office Ltd [2021] EWCA Crim 577

'They've been approaching this all wrong. It's not just a criminal case, it's a constitutional scandal and we need to treat it like one.' In December 2020 my colleague Lisa Busch QC and I took over the cases of Seema Misra, Tracy Felstead and Janet Skinner. They, along with twenty-three other former Post Office employees, were appealing against convictions dating back decades. In the 1990s, the Post Office, wholly owned by the government, installed a new accounting system called 'Horizon'. It was, at the time, the largest non-military system in Europe. Horizon recorded every transaction at every Post Office branch across the country and kept a record of profits, losses, stock and more. There was one problem: Horizon didn't work.

Before long Post Office workers started noticing errors; the day's takings didn't add up, stock totals were wrong. The system indicated there was more money in the till than was actually there. The Post Office management knew about these problems from the start. Rather than listening to its employees or investigating Horizon's shortcomings they accused employees of stealing. Hundreds of Post Office workers were prosecuted for theft, fraud and false accounting. Throughout the prosecutions, the Post Office claimed that Horizon was 'robust', concealing the quickly mounting pile of evidence of its flaws from the courts.[1]

In 2019 a civil court case revealed the problems with Horizon. The Criminal Cases Review Commission asked the Court of Appeal to review thirty-nine 'Horizon convictions', including those of my clients. It was instantly clear (and the Post Office conceded) that they did not have a fair trial, because prosecutors had concealed potentially exculpatory evidence. But the problems went deeper. Prosecutors (in this case the Post Office) have a duty to properly investigate all reasonable explanations. The Post Office, instead, had immediately blamed its own staff, placing on their shoulders the burden of proving their innocence. It used its enormous privilege to save face at the expense of the reputation, livelihoods and freedom of its workers. Not to mention their mental health – at least one person, Martin Griffiths, was driven to suicide.[2] This wasn't about a few errors in disclosure: one of the nation's most trusted institutions had flagrantly abused its powers.

In March 2021 we told the Court of Appeal that the Horizon prosecutions were 'an affront to the conscience of the court'. The judges agreed, concluding:

> the failures of investigation and disclosure were in our judgment so egregious as to make the prosecution of any of the

'Horizon cases' an affront to the conscience of the court . . .
POL effectively sought to reverse the burden of proof.

It overturned the convictions on the basis that the Post Office
had abused the court process, which was the most significant
finding of its kind in the UK's legal history.

The 'constitution' is the distribution of power between the
state and the citizens. In the UK, our constitution has a broadly
democratic direction. The balance of power permeates almost
every aspect of our day-to-day lives. My job, as a constitutional
lawyer, is to help set things right when the relationship between
citizens and the state becomes unbalanced or unjust. The Post
Office abused its powers as a public prosecutor. But the balance
can be upset by all manner of things; from a Prime Minister who
tries to rule without parliament to a Secretary of State who
keeps too many secrets, or even a local bureaucrat who goes
beyond their legal authority. Unfortunately, our constitution is
becoming ever more unbalanced and lawyers like me are increasingly unable to put things right.

When we talk about threats to democratic constitutions, we
often think of *coups d'état*. Western societies have a sort of collective smugness, assuming that no such thing could happen 'here'.
This was tested at the start of 2021 when domestic terrorists, at
the instigation of the outgoing President, stormed the US Capitol
building. The subject of this book, however, is a 'slow burn' crisis
whereby the norms and institutions that underpin our democratic constitution are undermined through a lengthy war of
attrition. As Harvard's Steven Levitsky and Daniel Ziblatt put it,
in their seminal study of the decline of modern democracies:

Blatant dictatorship . . . has disappeared across much of the
world. Military coups and other violent seizures of power are

rare . . . Democracies still die, but by different means. Since the end of the Cold War, most democratic breakdowns have been caused not by generals and soldiers but by elected governments themselves . . . Elected autocrats maintain a veneer of democracy while eviscerating its substance . . .

Because there is no single moment—no coup, declaration of martial law, or suspension of the constitution—in which the regime obviously 'crosses the line' into dictatorship, nothing may set off society's alarm bells. Those who denounce government abuse may be dismissed as exaggerating or crying wolf. Democracy's erosion is, for many, almost imperceptible.[3]

For those of us who spend our careers defending the UK's democratic constitution, Levitsky and Ziblatt's picture is unsettling. Since 2010, those in power have increasingly chipped away at the ideas and institutions that safeguard our interests. Some of these attacks, like the 2019 prorogation of parliament, are high-profile, capturing the imagination of the nation. Others are far more subtle. They are suffered initially by only a few individuals. Taken together, however, these start to feel like an avalanche.

Discussion of the problems within our democracy tends to focus on the Johnson government, as if this administration is somehow uniquely anti-democratic. Yet the Johnson government is merely symptomatic of a much deeper malaise. Our democratic crisis has been building for a long time. I've written this book to try and understand how we arrived here and what we can do about it.

We are reaching a tipping point: the democratic essentials have been cut back so far that we must ask how long Britain will remain a genuinely democratic state. Many of the matters discussed here will, taken alone, appear innocuous: the inevitable casualties of bareknuckle political competition, the realities of globalisation or the information age. I don't suggest that anything in this book, on its own, necessarily indicates a crisis. But it's all happening at the same time – and this is concerning.

The constitution is not about high principle debate between anxious academics and bewigged barristers. It is essential for effective government. As I wrote this book the UK suffered one of the worst coronavirus death rates in the world at the same time as one of the deepest pandemic recessions. Our ability to secure good government is so tenuous that the rest of the world is becoming cautious about lending Britain its money. In 2020 Moody's downgraded the UK's credit rating on the basis of a 'weakening in the UK's institutions and governance'.[4] It is the first time in history that this has occurred. Something is clearly wrong.

## The UK Constitution

The UK places ultimate political power in the hands of citizens and we lend it to our leaders through our representative institutions. Our government must act within the law and must remain accountable to citizens. Democratic accountability means more than periodic elections. As Abraham Lincoln put it, democracy is 'government by the people, for the people, and of the people'.[5] It's not just something we do on election day: it's a way of life. For democracy to work, power must be dispersed throughout society rather than concentrated in a small elite. We achieve this through principles like the rule of law, parliamentary sovereignty and the separation of powers. We rely on institutions such as parliament and the justice system to ensure that ordinary people exercise control over how we are governed. But we also need a society that embraces the right values: these include cherishing truth, critical thinking, respect for other viewpoints, individual rights and an appreciation that every individual is of equal worth.

But avenues of accountability have been closed down. The result is that unaccountable power is progressively concentrated in the hands of a select few. The UK is not alone in this regard. There is a disturbing international trend of formerly 'liberal democracies' becoming 'illiberal democracies' (illiberal democracy being arguably indistinguishable from autocracy). This is well documented in states like Hungary, Turkey and Brazil. In Britain we think of ourselves as exceptional, as somehow immune to the threats faced by other states. But our exceptionalism is imagined.

I witnessed the extent of our vulnerability through the cases I have argued. Representing a journalist against the Secretary of State, I saw how governments have dragged the UK towards unaccountable international institutions and treaties, blocked parliament from having a say in key decisions and given private lobbyists unparalleled access to foreign policy. Appearing for a local community against a major developer, I saw how, for many, the rights we take for granted have become almost meaningless. Acting on behalf of seventy-three MPs against the Prime Minister, I saw how our leaders are prepared to abandon any constitutional rule or custom to retain and amplify their power.

## Democracy

Four themes run through this book, with democracy as mother to all.

We often think of democracy as the 'foundation' of our constitution. It is better described, however, as the 'lodestar'. The UK constitution is, by nature, evolutionary. Just a few hundred years ago, we lived under something akin to an absolute monarchy. We achieved a democratic constitution because ordinary people wrestled power away from their erstwhile masters. Democracy is thus the direction of travel for our constitution, but we still have a long way to go. Society remains littered with hangovers from pre-democratic forms of government. They include the House of Lords, the relationship between the government and parliament, and the royal prerogative.

Our constitution is losing its lustre. We see this partly in our institutions and laws. Successive governments have used the vast power of the state to make it more difficult to oust them at election time, or to thwart the mechanisms that keep those in power accountable. Perhaps more worrying is that the way we understand democracy has changed. We have allowed principles that were once inviolable to become contestable. Most people now understand democracy as little more than crude majoritarianism. We're losing the fight for freedom in our own minds.

These issues will be explored through the four themes which run through this book. They are:

(1) Accountability
(2) Bullshit
(3) Centralisation
(4) Enfranchisement

*Accountability*

Power must ultimately lie with ordinary citizens. In practice, we delegate power to elected representatives (and, through them, to the government) to exercise on our behalf. But it must be loaned, not given. When we talk about 'accountability' we are talking about ensuring that those in power stick to the conditions of the loan.

This means we can demand our leaders change direction – or even replace them with someone else. This applies both to individual ministers and MPs and to the government and legislature as a whole. Accountability also means that when those with power misuse it, we are entitled to a remedy.

Accountability is a major casualty of our current crisis. Successive governments have eroded the mechanisms by which we keep them on their toes and we, as a nation, have allowed them to do so. Unless these decisions are reversed, and new and reformed avenues of accountability established, we run the risk that our conditional loan of power becomes an unconditional – and permanent – gift.

## Bullshit

Truth and transparency are of utmost importance to democracy. Our institutions and public discourse have, however, become infested with 'bullshit': statements which treat truth as immaterial.[6] The propensity of politicians to tell lies is nothing new, but we're ever more accepting of our leaders' deceptions. The dominance of bullshit in our national discourse has devalued truth as a social necessity and political norm.

In Chapter 2 I will examine what happens when political bullshit meets the forensic consideration of the courtroom. Bullshit will, however, appear in some form in every chapter because it infiltrates every aspect of society today.

## Centralisation

The third theme is centralisation of power. Both in the hands of government and of private individuals or groups. Throughout the last decade, government rhetoric has embraced the 'small state' (which David Cameron contrasted with the 'big society'). Government has consistently used the language of decentralisation. Claiming to empower local communities and free the UK from the bureaucratic behemoth of the EU. In reality, control has been increasingly centralised in Whitehall. Brexit has only fortified centralisation and bureaucracy.

Centralisation also refers to the gathering of political power in the hands of a small, unaccountable minority. This group overlaps with the government in Whitehall but is not exclusively the same. It includes media owners, party donors and other political influencers. Its members are able to exercise growing amounts of power through their control of the political process and national discourse.

## Enfranchisement

The real constitutional action, the sort that is meaningful and impactful over the long term, comes from us. Enfranchisement is both about how we, as individual citizens, can engage with power and how effectively we do so.

Our constitutional crisis will not be solved merely by legal or public policy reform. The only real remedy lies in the hands of the public. We must change the way we think about the constitution and what we are willing to accept and what we demand from our institutions, leaders and each other.

These four themes are inevitably co-dependent. The rise of bullshit makes accountability more difficult. Centralisation disenfranchises citizens. Our failure to properly use the rights that we have allows those most responsible for the chaos to get away with it. While each chapter will focus primarily on one theme, it will, in some way, speak to all of them.

This book is based on my experience as a lawyer. Many of the chapters tell the story of cases I have been involved in and which have exposed deep-seated issues. Some of these you may have heard about. Most, however, are not well known. But this does not make them any less important. I conclude with proposals to re-democratise our constitution; I do not pretend to have reached a complete solution. This book is intended to be the start of the debate, not its conclusion.

We each have our own window on the constitution. Mine is the courtroom. It is through the prism of my practice that I see how our constitution works or, more often than I'd like, doesn't. I don't pretend to be a constitutional scholar or any more expert than the thousands of my peers who, every day, work as I do. This book is just an attempt to share my own perspective. It will inevitably present an incomplete picture of the issues we face. The subject of race, for example, is mostly neglected and questions of devolution are underexplored. This is not because I don't think they are important; it is just that I have not conducted many cases in which these issues arose. Inevitably, as well, my courtroom victories may come across as righteous and my defeats unjust. I make no apologies for this. As a barrister I have an ethical obligation to only take on cases which I think are legally and factually justified. While some clients may push you to run bad points, you don't serve their interests by giving in. The best thing for a client with a bad case is to be advised to settle at the earliest possible stage. Running a loser just wastes the court's time and your client's money.

My approach is non-partisan. As Standing Counsel to the All-Party Parliamentary Group on the Constitution, I work with politicians of all stripes. Barristers have a principle called the 'cab rank rule'. This means that if I have the capacity and expertise to conduct a case, then I must accept the instruction regardless of my personal feelings. While I certainly have political opinions, I confine them to my personal life.

I don't propose, however, to muffle my conclusions in the name of non-partisanship. Where one side of the political debate is guilty of an attack against the constitution, I have no intention of pretending otherwise. The left of the political spectrum is often accused of 'authoritarianism'. The inescapable conclusion, however, from the events related in this book is that many meaningful attacks on our constitution come from the right.

Why do I identify the last decade as a period of building constitutional crisis? All governments chafe at the bonds of the constitution. Tony Blair, for example, pursued 'surveillance state' policies that were problematic. But Blair was forced to step back from his most egregious assaults on democratic rights (like the imposition of ID cards). He bowed to pressure from the public and, in part, from his own MPs. The guardrails of the constitution were tested but held. Since 2010, however, those guardrails have fallen away.

Discussions of these highly charged and polarising issues can too easily devolve into hysteria. One needs to spend only a few moments on Twitter to see the most innocuous opinions placed on the same level as those of Hitler and Genghis Khan. This book is therefore about the journey we have taken as a society, from (almost absolute) monarchy to an imperfect form of democracy. It is about how, during the last decade, the direction of travel has wavered and perhaps reversed. The risk we face as a nation is not that we will turn into Nazi Germany but that we will turn into a past, less democratic, version of ourselves.

# 1

# THE LODESTAR OF
# THE CONSTITUTION

*Let us remind ourselves of the foundations of our
constitution. We live in a representative democracy.
The House of Commons exists because the people
have elected its members . . . The Government exists
because it has the confidence of the House of
Commons. It has no democratic legitimacy other than
that.*

Lady Hale, *Miller/Cherry v
Prime Minister* [2020] AC 373

On 28 August 2019 three government ministers raced a court
messenger to Balmoral Castle. Literally raced. The ministers
were admitted, met with the Queen and came out with the
authority to close down parliament.[1] The messenger was blocked
by armed guards. Had he been allowed past the gates he would
have informed Her Majesty that the ministers' advice was
unlawful. Less than a month later, the Supreme Court would
confirm this message.

Thus began the cases of *Cherry v Advocate General* (in
Scotland) and *Miller v the Prime Minister (No. 2)* (in England),

collectively known as 'the prorogation case'. In Scotland, the Court of Session (the Scottish Court of Appeal) found the prorogation unlawful. In England, the High Court disagreed. The Supreme Court was asked to break the deadlock.[2] It had to look into the very heart of our constitution and answer two fundamental questions: is the UK a democracy and, if so, what does that entail?

In June 2016 the UK voted to leave the EU, kicking off a two-year negotiation about the terms of exit. The government said it would be the 'easiest negotiation in history'.[3]

Two years later there was still no agreement. During the referendum Brexit campaigners insisted that 'absolutely no one' was advocating a 'no-deal Brexit'.[4] Nevertheless, in the summer of 2019, the government began to consider doing just that.

Parliament couldn't agree on what it wanted. But it was very clear about what it didn't want: a no-deal Brexit. Accordingly, when no agreement was reached in the spring of 2019, parliament forced the May government to seek a series of extensions to the Brexit deadline until 31 October 2019.

In response, a small number of hard-right MPs, commentators and think tanks suggested that the UK should embrace a no-deal Brexit. If parliament didn't like it, parliament should be closed down ('prorogued') until Brexit was accomplished.[5]

The last British leader to shutter a parliament because it disagreed with him was Charles I (in 1629), so this proposal met with some raised eyebrows. For Matt Hancock, it went 'against everything those men who waded onto those beaches [during the Normandy Landings] fought and died for – and I will not have it'. For Sajid Javid, it was 'trashing democracy'. For Michael Gove, it 'would not be true to the best traditions of British democracy'.[6] Nevertheless, in the summer of 2019 the new Prime Minister, Boris Johnson, began putting together a plan to prorogue and Hancock, Javid and Gove, all given jobs in Johnson's cabinet, made no complaint.

That's where I came in. MPs didn't want to shut down parliament but Johnson did it anyway. Legislators had no option but to ask the courts to step in. A cross-party coalition of seventy-eight parliamentarians from across the UK did just that. They were led by Joanna Cherry QC MP, the SNP's justice spokesperson, and coordinated by Jolyon Maugham QC, the Director of the Good Law Project (an NGO which brings legal claims in the public interest).

I joined their legal team in July. We were led by Aidan O'Neill QC, a legend of the public law bar. The claim would begin in Scotland (in the Court of Session) but concerned UK-wide issues. Aidan was, therefore, to be assisted by two junior barristers, one qualified in Scots law (David Welsh) and one in English law (me).[7]

The government beat us to the punch. Johnson sent his ministers to Balmoral before the courts could determine the legality of his plan, the Queen confirmed his decision to prorogue and Johnson quickly dismissed parliament. The prorogation prevented legislators from scrutinising his Brexit negotiations and allowed him to rule by fiat for at least five weeks. It was the longest prorogation (without a general election) in more than half a century.[8] For the first time since 1629 (when Charles I ruled without parliament for eleven years, sparking the English Civil War), the executive had used the power of prorogation to prevent MPs from blocking its agenda.

At this point the legal fight began in earnest. My task was to distil exactly how Johnson's prorogation stuck a knife into the heart of British values. Aidan's advice: start with Robert the Bruce.

## The Road to Enlightenment

I wanted to put a simple proposition before the court: 'the UK is a democratic country. This means the government cannot arbitrarily dismiss the representatives of the people.' But it was never going to be that easy. 'Democracy' means different things to different people. Unlike the US constitution, which was written down in one fell swoop, the UK constitution is as much a journey as an entity. It has evolved, as a body of law and principle, as we have evolved as a society.

The courts have long recognised this. As the Judicial Committee of the House of Lords (the predecessor to the Supreme Court) observed in 1995:

> The constitutional history of this country is the history of the prerogative powers of the Crown being made subject to the overriding powers of the democratically elected legislature as the sovereign body.[9]

There was nothing inevitable about this. We as citizens repeatedly chose to move in a democratic direction and demanded the same from our leaders. I needed to tell the story of how the UK reached this point in our constitutional history and how our understanding of democracy developed along the way.

After becoming King of Scots in 1306 Robert the Bruce defeated both Edward II and Edward III to end English overlordship of Scotland. Unusually for a medieval monarch, however, he did not claim a divine right to rule. His kingship, in his own words, rested on the 'due consent and assent' of his subjects. Should he betray the trust of those he ruled, they reserved the right to choose someone else. Political legitimacy in Bruce's Scotland thus flowed from the agreement of the people (or at least a portion of them). In other words, Bruce recognised that he was king because his people had made a choice. This early flowering of democratic ideas, however, was the exception rather than the norm. For the majority of their history, England, Scotland and Wales (both individually and as 'the UK') have been ruled by kings and queens 'as of right'.

In the late medieval and early modern periods England approached something akin to an absolute monarchy. Power flowed primarily from the monarch and the vast majority of people were subjugated. From the mid-seventeenth century, the aristocracy began to pry power away from the monarch, but this did not mean that power was shared with ordinary people. Political power was held almost solely by a small group of aristocrats and oligarchs until well into the nineteenth century. Indeed, it was not until the middle of the twentieth century that the majority of people in the UK were allowed to vote.

All versions of the non-democratic constitutions were justified by the same underlying logic: people are not of equal value. As Henry Ireton told the Putney Debates in 1647: 'most people' were 'of small substance and no value'. More than two hundred years later, Walter Bagehot, the editor of the *Economist*, warned that allowing too many people to vote would empower 'the lower orders' who 'are equally despotic [as their masters], but are not equally intelligent'.[10] Even by 1957, Earl Ferrers was able to argue against the admission of women to the House of Lords:

> Frankly, I find women in politics highly distasteful. In general, they are organising, they are pushing, and they are commanding. Some of them do not even know where their loyalty to their country lies . . . It is generally accepted, for better or worse, that a man's judgment is generally more logical and less tempestuous than that of a woman. Why then should we encourage women

to eat their way, like acid into metal, into positions of trust and responsibility which previously men have held?[11]

We moved, as a society, towards democracy because we chose to accept that all people are of equal value. I call this 'the equality principle'. We still have a long way to go. It's fair to say, however, that by the end of the twentieth century a critical mass of people accepted the basic 'rightness' of the equality principle, and it was embedded within our law and discourse.

The journey to this point was a long one. Medieval monarchs governed on the basis of 'divine right'. As James I of England (and VI of Scotland) put it in 1610:

> The state of monarchy is the supremest thing upon earth; for kings are not only God's lieutenants upon earth, and sit upon God's throne, but even by God himself are called gods ... [Kings are] judges over all their subjects and in all causes and yet accountable to none but God only.[12]

Britain was never an 'absolutist' monarchy like France or Prussia. For much of the Middle Ages power fluctuated between the monarch, various groups of barons and the church. From 1485 the Tudor monarchs built a more central-ised state, establishing the crown as the supreme power. While their successors, the Stuarts, are most associated with claims to 'divine right', they mainly repeated ideas that had existed for centuries.[13]

Parliament existed during this time, but not in the form we recognise today. The monarch summoned a parliament, demanded it grant taxes, then dismissed it as soon as its 'duty' was done. Parliament comprised the nobility and the 'commons'. The former sat, by right of birth, in the House of Lords. Almost all seats in 'the House of Commons' were controlled by members of the nobility and awarded to their retainers.[14]

Even under such monarchical rule, however, we can see the seeds of liberalism. The Peasants' Revolt in 1381 was arguably the first mass movement around ideas recognisable to modern democrats. Thousands of peasants and artisans marched on London. Despite the dangers that faced anyone who challenged the medieval regime, they demanded (what would now be called) civil and political rights. Addressing the 'army' assembled at Blackheath, John Ball identified the essence of democracy:

> Are we not all descended from the same parents, Adam and Eve? And what can they show, or what reasons give, why they should be more the masters than ourselves? Except, perhaps, in making us labour and work, for them to spend.[15]

The Peasants' Revolt was brutally suppressed. But the embers of democracy continued to smoulder. During the English Civil War parliament deposed and executed Charles I because he refused to share power. In the aftermath of the war the parliamentary army met at Putney to debate the future constitution. Thomas Rainsborough told the Putney Debates:

> I think that the poorest he that is in England hath a life to live, as the greatest he; and therefore truly, sir, I think it's clear, that every man that is to live under a government ought first by his own consent to put himself under that government.[16]

Rainsborough, like Ball, articulated the equality principle. But his proposal was rejected. Oliver Cromwell became 'Lord Protector' and effectively ruled as king until his death. Shortly thereafter parliament and the army invited Charles I's son (Charles II) to return to the throne. Charles II was succeeded by his brother, James II. Like his father and grandfather, James had pretensions to rule by divine right. As a result, he was deposed by parliament in 1688 ('the Glorious Revolution') and William of Orange was invited to take the throne, but only on the conditions set down in the Bill of Rights 1688.

The Civil War and the Glorious Revolution did not establish a constitution in the manner envisaged by Rainsborough (or understood today). They did, however, refute the 'divine right of kings'. After 1688 the monarch, as a matter of fact, held the throne only because they had been invited to do so by parliament. They exercised power only within the bounds that parliament had permitted. The electorate was entitled to a choice in how they were governed (even if, at this stage, it was largely symbolic).

But parliament itself could not, for much of the seventeenth to nineteenth centuries, be called 'democratic'. The vast majority of people remained excluded from political life. Indeed, the very idea of 'democracy' was considered a threat to the nation, equivalent to treason. Nevertheless, democratic ideas continued to emerge, built on versions of the equality principle. In the seventeenth century, philosophers like John Locke argued that 'nature' made all 'men' fundamentally equal and, consequently, all 'men' had an equal right to determine who governed them. A hundred years later, political theorists like Thomas Paine insisted that all people have inherent 'natural' rights.[19] Jeremy Bentham and John Stuart Mill proposed that government be conducted in the interests of the whole of society. Mill set out how this could be ensured in practice through the rule of law and universal suffrage.

The ideas of the Enlightenment philosophers were promulgated by a press which, if not free, was difficult for the government to control. 'Radical' (anti-authoritarian) figures like William Cobbett, John Bright, Richard Cobden and (later) David Lloyd George obtained seats in parliament and a national platform for their views. As the nineteenth century progressed, citizens increasingly demanded a say in government. Reformers like Henry Hunt drew mass crowds to their rallies for reform, and the Chartist movement insisted on the sort of political rights that we now recognise as essential to a modern democratic state.[20] The suffrage movement and the nascent Labour Party demanded votes and civil liberties.

Throughout the UK's evolution, however, the proponents of reform were brutally repressed. From the 1790s to the 1810s the government of William Pitt the Younger prosecuted the 'English Terror' against suspected democrats. Many, including Thomas Paine, were convicted of treason for the crime of advocating democratic ideas. Some were executed. The government whipped up 'Church and King' mobs to harass and assault supporters of constitutional reform. Lord Braxfield (one of Scotland's most senior judges), summing up in the trial of Thomas Muir (charged with treason for distributing Paine's writing), exemplified the establishment's attitude:

> the defendant had gone among ignorant country people making them forget their work, and telling them that a reform of the franchise was absolutely necessary for preserving their liberty. What right, he asked, had they to representation? A government in every country should be just like a corporation, and in Britain it was made up of the landed interest who alone had a right to be represented.[21]

In the nineteenth century the army was regularly used to break up public meetings in support of political rights. Often, as at the

Peterloo massacre[22] and Bullring 'riot',[23] soldiers and police murdered or assaulted unarmed attendees. Women campaigning for the right to vote were beaten and sexually assaulted by police when they demonstrated peacefully; when their demonstrations became violent they were tortured in prison.[24] Trade unions were outlawed as was any organisation promoting 'radical' politics (i.e. any challenge to the status quo). Britain only moved in a democratic direction because such 'radicals' persisted despite repression, harassment and intimidation. Eventually, the majority of the population joined them. From the early nineteenth century, parliament began to make itself more accountable by extending the franchise (albeit initially only to a small number of wealthy men). But it took another hundred years before the ship of state began consistently to navigate by the lodestar of democracy.

The Parliament Acts of 1909 and 1949 established the primacy of the (elected) Commons over the (unelected) Lords. The Representation of the People Acts established universal suffrage. In the early years of the twenty-first century the Blair government's reforms of the House of Lords finally limited the legislative power of the aristocracy.

The latter part of the twentieth century also saw efforts to reduce the repression of minority groups (the Sexual Offences Act 1967 and the Race Relations Act 1976). The equality principle was given practical effect by the European Convention on Human Rights, the Human Rights Act 1998 and the Equality Act 2010. These instruments empowered citizens to insist that the government treat them as having equal value, and to seek remedies when it failed to do so.

Discrimination against minority groups has not been eliminated. And shades of the monarchic and oligarchic constitutions still haunt public life. The House of Lords, for example, remains a mixture of peers appointed by the Prime Minister and hereditary aristocrats. Much of government is conducted in secret, away from the inconvenience of public scrutiny.[25] And our electoral system is structured so that a party can win a majority of seats in the House of Commons without winning a majority of the votes cast in the election.

Nevertheless, by the end of the twentieth century, the equality principle was generally accepted by most people. As Baroness Hale (who would later preside over the prorogation case as President of the Supreme Court) recognised in 2004:

> Democracy is founded on the principle that each individual has equal value. Treating some as automatically having less value than others not only causes pain and distress to that person but also violates his or her dignity as a human being . . . Democracy values everyone equally even if the majority does not.[26]

## The Constitution Today

The equality principle was at the heart of the prorogation case. It requires that government must be conducted according to the law, and the law cannot be made but with the consent of the governed. Parliament was the supreme governing institution, but only because it exercised the democratic mandate. As Lord Hope observed, in *Jackson v The Attorney General* (2006):

> It must never be forgotten that this rule [that only parliament may make law] . . . depends upon the legislature maintaining the trust of the electorate. In a democracy the need of the elected members to maintain this trust is a vitally important safeguard. The principle of parliamentary sovereignty . . . is built upon the

assumption that Parliament represents the people whom it exists to serve.[27]

The other constitutional institutions are the executive ('the government') and the judiciary. The executive is charged with the day-to-day government of the country and with implementing the laws passed by parliament. Under the monarchical constitution the executive comprised the ministers appointed by the monarch. Formally, at least, that is still the case. In practice, however, the monarch asks the person best able to command a majority in the House of Commons to form a government. This person becomes Prime Minister. The prorogation case came about because the Prime Minister abused his powers. Lady Hale reminded the government of its constitutional place:

> Let us remind ourselves of the foundations of our constitution. *We live in a representative democracy.* The House of Commons exists because the people have elected its members. The Government is not directly elected by the people (unlike the position in some other democracies). The Government exists because it has the confidence of the House of Commons. It has no democratic legitimacy other than that. This means that it is accountable to the House of Commons – and indeed to the House of Lords – for its actions, remembering always that the actual task of governing is for the executive and not for Parliament or the courts.[28]

The judiciary comprises the judges and the court system. The judges are appointed by an independent, non-partisan panel based on merit. Judges who sit in the Court of Appeal and Supreme Court have, therefore, been tested extensively throughout their careers and proven both their expertise and deep understanding of the law. The role of the judiciary is to enforce the laws set down by parliament and the common law. They ensure that the Prime Minister is no more able to break the law than anyone else. The judiciary does not make law and it does not take sides in politics. It is concerned solely with interpreting and enforcing the law. The courts are ultimately subject to the legislature. If parliament believes that a court has decided a case wrongly then it can legislate to change the law in future.

The prorogation case was a test of the respective roles of the three branches of the constitution. In proroguing parliament, the executive had prevented the legislature from fulfilling one of its constitutional roles. The judiciary therefore had to exercise its own constitutional function and put an end to the Prime Minister's law breaking.

Judges make decisions by examining the established law and applying it to the new set of facts before them. By the early twenty-first century our constitutional law was contained in statutes (laws made by parliament), common law 'constitutional principles' (general rules accepted as necessary for the practical functioning of our politics), 'constitutional conventions' and various practices left over from pre-democratic days. Two such legacies of our undemocratic past were of particular importance to the prorogation case.

The first, 'the Royal Prerogative', is a hangover from the days of medieval monarchy. Prerogative powers were once held by medieval monarchs. They are the 'rump' powers which were not stripped from the monarch by parliament.[29] These powers are now generally exercised by ministers on the monarch's behalf. The power to prorogue parliament is a prerogative power. This, for me, summed up the absurdity of the situation: the Johnson government had used powers left over from the 'divine right'

25

monarchy to do away with parliament. In a genuine democracy, there is no case for allowing prerogative powers to exist at all, let alone to be used to silence the elected representatives of the people.[30]

The second hangover in the prorogation case, 'constitutional conventions', harks back to the days of seventeenth- and eighteenth-century oligarchy. Constitutional conventions are 'political morality'; informal agreements which purport to secure constitutional rights.[31] The government argued that the exercise of the prorogation prerogative was governed solely by constitutional convention. Traditionally, the executive was trusted not to abuse the prerogative power so the court should trust them not to do so now.

## Accountability: Turning Theory Into Reality

The government's lawyers sought to wind the clock back to a time before executives were subject to the law. They argued that prorogation was a 'political' question and that only parliament could hold the government to account. Their case did not survive first contact with reality. Parliament, being prorogued, cannot un-prorogue itself. The only body to which, according to its lawyers, the government owed any responsibility, had already been closed down. It was a legal argument on a par with 'Catch-22'.

The government's case forced us to grapple with another constitutional concept: accountability. You can have all the constitutional rules, principles and statutes you like but if ordinary citizens can't make sure the government complies we may as well not have a constitution at all. Accountability, therefore, turns constitutional theory into constitutional reality.

In the UK we primarily hold power to account in two ways.

On questions of politics and policy we hold the government accountable through parliament (i.e. we elect MPs and they hold the government to account on our behalf). On questions of law, we hold the government to account through the courts. Prorogation was a question of law: had the Prime Minister acted within the scope of his power to prorogue?

We responded to the government's case with three points. First, the fact that the case would have political consequences didn't make it a 'purely political' matter. The court's job was to adjudicate on the law. If the government had broken the law then the court must rule against it, regardless of any political embarrassment to ministers. Second, the courts and parliament have different constitutional roles. Parliament makes law and the courts determine whether that law has been broken. If the government had acted unlawfully, it must answer to the courts. Third, the government's case would mean that it could prorogue parliament whenever it wanted to avoid parliamentary scrutiny. This clearly violated democratic constitutional principles.

The Supreme Court agreed with us on all three. Having determined that the question was justiciable (i.e. one that was appropriate for the court to answer), the judges went on to determine whether the government had acted unlawfully. Clearly prorogation is not, in and of itself, unlawful. The government has the power to prorogue and is entitled to use it. But it can't go beyond the extent of its power or use it unlawfully. The question for the court, therefore, was whether the power to prorogue could be used in any way the government wanted or whether it was limited by constitutional principle. In particular, could the power be used with the effect of preventing scrutiny of the final phases of the Brexit negotiations?

The Supreme Court relied on two key constitutional

principles: parliamentary sovereignty and parliamentary accountability. As Lady Hale described them:

> The first is the principle of Parliamentary sovereignty: that laws enacted by the Crown in Parliament are the supreme form of law in our legal system, with which everyone, including the Government, must comply . . . prerogative powers are limited by the principle of Parliamentary sovereignty.
>
> . . .
>
> The same question arises in relation to a second constitutional principle, that of Parliamentary accountability . . . As Lord Bingham of Cornhill said in the case of *Bobb v Manning* [2006] UKPC 22 at [13] the conduct of government by a Prime Minister and Cabinet collectively responsible and accountable to Parliament lies at the heart of Westminster democracy . . . the policies of the executive are subjected to consideration by the representatives of the electorate . . . and citizens are protected from the arbitrary exercise of executive power.[33]

At this point the case became very simple: obviously the prorogation ran contrary to the principles of parliamentary sovereignty and accountability. Parliament can't hold the executive accountable if the executive can send it home whenever things get a bit controversial.

The court accepted that sometimes it may be necessary for parliament to be prorogued for longer periods (such as in a time of war). It therefore had to consider whether the prorogation had a 'reasonable justification'. According to the government, it needed to introduce a number of new bills to parliament and could not do so unless the current session was ended and a new one begun. As Lady Hale pointed out, however, the government could have achieved this aim with a prorogation lasting a few days. There was no reasonable justification for a prorogation which lasted five weeks. The case was over. We had won.

More importantly, we had re-established a key principle of the democratic constitution: that the government could not rule without the consent of (and accountability to) the governed. Unfortunately, as we were about to be reminded, just as we are capable of establishing democratic norms so we are capable of abandoning them. The next chapter will explore the aftermath of the prorogation case and the sustained attack on one of our most important democratic principles: truth.

# 2

# LIES, DAMN LIES
# AND BULLSHIT

> *The circumstances demonstrate that [contrary to the government's submissions] the true reason for the prorogation is to reduce the time available for Parliamentary scrutiny of Brexit.*
>
> Lord Carloway, Cherry v
> Advocate General [2019] CSIH 49

The conclusion of a big case can be slightly anti-climactic. For weeks, months or years you have been 'in the eye of the hurricane'.* Every decision you take feels momentous. When you get to court all eyes are on you. An expectant hush descends when leading counsel stands to address the Bench. We juniors live and die with our leader as they present the arguments that we have spent many sleepless nights developing. Then, all of a sudden, it's over.

After Lady Hale finished her judgment, Joanna, Gina (Miller) and Jolyon emerged from court to the cheers of supporters and the clamour of the waiting press. The rest of us found ourselves

---

* With apologies to Lin-Manuel Miranda.

standing, slightly awkwardly, in the court doorway. Eventually Elaine Motion, our solicitor, suggested we go to lunch. We slipped off through a side exit and found a taxi.

Crammed together in the back of the cab, we listened as the radio, tuned to LBC, broadcast the court's decision. I couldn't resist grinning at Elaine. But my elation caught in my throat. The cabbie (recognising us from our brief appearances in the background of various news reports) turned around to face us. He said, 'The British people will never forgive you for what you've done.'

Almost immediately the case took on a whole new meaning in the public eye. Our attempt to restore parliament was reframed as an assault. The court's decision, which scrupulously avoided taking sides in the political debate, was cast as a despotic power grab. Judges were 'interfering' in politics and defying the 'will of the people'. The prorogation case became a microcosm of a public discourse that is increasingly detached from reality.

This chapter explores the second major theme of the book: bullshit.

The Supreme Court had struck down an attack on the constitution. In the aftermath, the government and its allies launched an attack on the constitution's most important moral value: truth. It's a value that dates back at least to the beginning of the eighth century. What became England was then divided into multiple smaller kingdoms which warred alternately with each other and waves of Viking invaders. Alfred the Great is the best-known ruler of the southern kingdom of Wessex. But it was his grandson Athelstan who first ruled a state recognisable as 'England'. In the early tenth century he issued the first national body of law: the Dooms of Athelstan.

The Dooms focus primarily on property and criminal law. A pervading theme, however, is the sanctity of truth. Athelstan decreed that the punishment for lying would not only last a life-time but would continue after death:

> if it be found that any of these have given wrongful witness, that his witness never again be believed . . .
>
> And he who shall swear a false oath, and it be made clear against him; that he never after be oath-worthy, nor let him lie within a hallowed burial-place, though he die . . .[1]

Even under the 'divine right' of monarchs, truth remained an essential civic value. Our constitutional edifices were built on its foundation.

Public discourse is essential to democracy and truth is essential to public discourse. In ancient Athens the 'citizens' would gather together to discuss the needs of the *polis*, share ideas and debate opinions.[2] In revolutionary America James Madison saw the public space as vital, even where it was not possible for citizens to gather in the same physical space. If government gains its authority from the governed, then the latter must have a space in which to work out their collective views. This can be the Athenian forum, the newspapers, the debating chambers of the fourteen colonies, or even Twitter. In the modern UK the 'public space' is a metaphor for all the many fora in which we can exchange ideas. It thus exists both online and offline, in person and remotely. It may be overtly political or cultural, philosophical or even just gossipy.[3]

Public discourse plays a particularly important role in the UK. The force of public pressure (whether communicated directly or through our elected representatives) polices the constitution and keeps those in power honest.

In the prorogation case we overturned the government's wrongdoing but we could not do anything to prevent the same thing from happening again. The courts cannot fire or fine ministers. Even parliament's powers of censure are relatively limited. Much relies on ministers understanding their error and 'doing the right thing'. In court we exposed the Prime Minister. We revealed how he tried to dispense with the elected parliament when it got in the way of his plans and then lied to the country about it. His predecessor, Theresa May, resigned after parliament rejected her withdrawal agreement. Johnson tried (and failed) to shutter parliament itself.

Yet public pressure for Johnson to resign was minimal. Listening to the prevailing winds of public discourse in October 2019 was to believe that the real threat to our constitution did not come from the executive, which had tried to govern without parliament, but rather from those who restored the representatives of the people to their rightful place.

This is just one example of a public discourse that is no longer fit for purpose. Ipsos MORI runs regular surveys asking respondents to state what they believe to be true about various public issues and compares their responses with the facts. Over the last decade these have consistently shown a substantial gap between what most people believe and what is actually true.[4] As the *Independent* put it: the 'British public [is] wrong about nearly everything'.[5] If our public discourse is not grounded *mostly* in reality, then we cannot operate effectively as a nation.

## Bullshit

Our public discourse is increasingly dominated by what Professor Harry Frankfurt calls 'bullshit'.[6] For Frankfurt, 'bullshit' is a discourse which seeks to persuade without regard for the truth. Frankfurt distinguishes 'bullshit' from simply 'lying'. A liar implicitly acknowledges the truth by subverting it.

A bullshitter has no regard for the truth whatsoever. Bullshit is about getting your version of events out before your opponent's. Bullshit statements may contain a kernel of truth, they may be outright lies, misrepresentations or straw men or they can simply take other statements out of context. To the bullshitter, it doesn't matter.

Frankfurt says bullshit has always been present in public discourse. From the 1980s and 1990s, however, as the volume and intensity of communications increased so did the incentive to bullshit. People were expected to have more opinions and there were more platforms available to share their thoughts with others. Many of us, under pressure to keep up, increasingly turned to bullshit.[7]

In the last decade two things have changed. First, the rise of social media means it is easier to spread the bullshit around. Second, political leaders have increasingly adopted bullshit discourses. This normalises bullshit and decreases the social value of truth. Government ministers now enthusiastically spout bullshit in public without consequence. In May 2018 Jacob Rees-Mogg told *Daily Politics*:

> If you are in a negotiation for a free trade agreement, you can maintain your existing standards for ten years under WTO rules. So we have ten years from the point at which we leave the European Union to negotiate a free trade agreement with the EU which would mean we can carry on with our zero tariffs.[8]

This was, in the words of a trade lawyer friend, 'utter bollocks'. It was, however, 'utter bollocks' spouted by a leading politician (who was subsequently rewarded with a cabinet post) on one of the BBC's flagship shows. By the time anyone could correct Rees-Mogg's statement, the damage had been done.

Few politicians have reaped the rewards of bullshit more than Boris Johnson. When we began the prorogation case, Johnson fell back on bullshit, writing to MPs to explain his decision:

> The current session has lasted more than 340 days and needs to be brought to a close – in almost 400 years only the 2010–12 session comes close, at 250 days.
>
> Bills have been introduced, which, while worthy in their own right, have at times seemed more about filling time in both the Commons and the Lords, while key Brexit legislation has been held back to ensure it could still be considered for carry-over into a second session.[9]

This story was met with incredulity. Johnson's allies had been publicly discussing using prorogation to block parliament since January 2019.[10]

The government's explanation was a classic example of bullshit. The real reason was veiled. The story, however, contained a kernel of truth: parliament *had* sat for a long time and it *was* necessary to prorogue to make way for a Queen's Speech. There was just enough to provoke a debate. But these factual statements were used to mislead.

The courtroom is one of the few public spaces that continues to both value and depend on the truth. When we came before the Inner House, the irresistible force of Johnson's bullshit met the immovable object of Scots judicial scepticism. Lord Carloway saw through the government's story:

> The circumstances demonstrate that the true reason for the prorogation is to reduce the time available for Parliamentary scrutiny of Brexit at a time when such scrutiny would appear to

be a matter of considerable importance, given the issues at stake.[11]

Unfortunately, not every public statement can be forensically tested under the eagle eye of a judge. Truth is inherently democratic: anyone can tell the truth. If public discourse is just about getting your message to as many people as possible then those with the biggest platform (rather than the best arguments) have an overwhelming advantage. Newspaper owners, government ministers and those able to pay to promote their views are more likely to persuade people than the rest of us. The more bullshit becomes socially acceptable, the more it becomes the case that 'power is truth'.

Peter Oborne, in his book *Assault on Truth*, argues that Boris Johnson and Donald Trump are uniquely mendacious.[12] Yet UK governments have been embracing bullshit since at least 2010. The Cameron coalition and its tabloid allies flooded the public arena with stories claiming the previous government's support for 'skivers' had caused the 2007 economic crash. Tabloid headlines, ministerial speeches and political ads told stories of communities in which four generations had never worked. Most turned out to be entirely false. Yet they permeated the public consciousness and propped up public support for austerity even as it made millions poorer and less secure.[13]

In the 2015 general election Cameron's Conservative Party ran a billboard campaign portraying Ed Miliband as (literally) in the pocket of SNP leader Alex Salmond. Yet Miliband opposed Scottish independence, ruled out a coalition government with the SNP and was fighting a bloody political war with Salmond's party in Scotland. Nevertheless, as one strategist claimed afterwards, the bullshit advert helped the governing party retain power.[14]

In the 2019 general election government press officers briefed that a party aide had been 'punched in the face' by an opposition activist outside Leeds General Infirmary. The BBC's political editor Laura Kuenssberg tweeted the story and it was quickly picked up by the BBC, ITV and most mainstream news websites. It was not long before a video emerged debunking the story. By that time, however, the bullshit had done its job. The story had been read or watched hundreds of thousands of times and shared on social media hundreds of thousands of times more.[15] It didn't matter that it wasn't true, it mattered that lots of people believed it.

The flood of bullshit is no coincidence; it's a deliberate decision taken by politicians. Conservative activists are now encouraged to 'weaponise fake news', in order to ensure 'honest politicians' are 'pushed off the front pages' (the same instruction may have been given to Labour activists but there is no evidence of this).[16] In the 2021 London mayoral election we saw this strategy in practice. The Conservative candidate, Shaun Bailey, sent Londoners letters which purported to be from the sitting Mayor (Labour's Sadiq Khan) informing them of a 21% tax rise.[17] Khan had made no such proposal but by the time it was debunked Bailey's campaign had enjoyed a whole news cycle of 'tax rise' stories.

## Invented Enemies

Some bullshit tropes are so well established that they are used over and over again. One of the most common is the invented enemy. The public discourse is refocused from real issues towards an imaginary enemy, a group or force which can be blamed for the problems facing the country.

In the aftermath of the prorogation case the new invented

enemy became lawyers, judges and anyone seeking to challenge the government in court. The Government Legal Department employs 2,600 staff, including 1,900 lawyers. They are supported by a network of independent counsel, consultants, solicitors and other services at a cost of more than £20 million every year.[18] Joanna Cherry's legal team comprised nine people. All of us acted pro bono. It came as something of a surprise, therefore, to find out that I was not David, but Goliath. We were apparently part of a 'liberal elite' which was 'a danger to the country'.[19] I couldn't help but feel that if I was a member of 'the elite' then I would at least have been paid. The narrative was clear: the Johnson government was the lone warrior, fighting for the nation against a perfidious 'liberal elite' intent on overturning the 'will of the people'. Johnson's attempt to close down parliament became an act of patriotism.

The invented enemy has been a feature of British public discourse for over a century. In the nineteenth century the 'enemy' was the Irish (then still a colonised people occupied by Britain). As Benjamin Disraeli, in a speech shortly before becoming a member of parliament, said:

[the Irish] hate our order, our civilisation, our enterprising industry, our religion. This wild, reckless, indolent, uncertain and superstitious race have no sympathy with the English character.[20]

In the first part of the twentieth century the Irish were joined by the Jews. They were accused of 'undercutting the wages of indigenous labour, stealing jobs and straining the already overburdened housing stock'.[21] (The nature of these accusations may be familiar to some.)

After the Jews came the communists. By the 1920s, fear of

communist 'infiltration' was so strong that it helped bring down the (Labour) MacDonald government. A letter purporting to be from Grigory Zinoviev (the president of the Russian-controlled Communist International) was leaked to the *Daily Mail*. It called on British communists to mobilise 'sympathetic forces' in the Labour Party. To many it seemed to be a 'smoking gun', exposing a conspiracy among the political left to sell Britain out to the 'red menace' overseas. The Labour Party, unsurprisingly, lost the 1924 election. But the Zinoviev letter was a fake. It was leaked by supporters of the Conservative Party in the security services. One of the (real) conspirators, Major Joseph Ball, joined Conservative Central Office in 1926.[22]

The dominant invented enemies of recent years are immigrants. They are, if the discourse is to be believed, the reason for almost all of our woes. They cause lower wages (because immigrants will work for less), fewer jobs and a loss of 'Britishness' (whatever that is). Politicians of all stripes have jumped on the bandwagon, promising ever more aggressive measures to 'tackle' immigration. Immigrants are incredibly convenient scapegoats. They often lack voting rights, representation in the media and the funds to 'answer back' through think tanks and lobbyists. Immigrants are, to today's bullshitters, what Jews were to those of the early twentieth century.

The irony of invented enemies is that when faced with a real crisis, like the Covid-19 pandemic, government is left completely unprepared. The Johnson government's response proved so incompetent that even its media allies began to desert it. An editorial in *The Times*, entitled 'The Times view on the prime minister's suitability for No 10', captured the mood in the country in September 2020:

> Too often the government has over-promised and under-delivered on the testing programme, the tracking app, schools reopening and others besides.[23]

This is, in retrospect, entirely predictable. When public discourse has, for a decade, obsessed over enemies that don't really exist, it is unsurprising that government hasn't developed the capability to respond to one that does.

## Appropriated Victimhood

Appropriated victimhood is one of the most insidious forms of bullshit. It involves a powerful person or organisation covering up abuses of power by pretending to be a victim. Lady Hale's judgment in the prorogation case was studiedly non-political. It began:

> It is important to emphasise that the issue in these appeals is not when and on what terms the United Kingdom is to leave the European Union. The issue is whether the advice given by the Prime Minister to Her Majesty the Queen on 27 or 28 August 2019 that Parliament should be prorogued from a date between 9 and 12 September until 14 October was lawful.[24]

Despite Lady Hale's clarity, the government and its allies adopted an attitude of wounded bewilderment, claiming to be the victims of judicial overreach rather than the law breakers that the court had found them to be. Jacob Rees-Mogg affected bafflement. The government had done nothing wrong. The Supreme Court had enacted a 'constitutional coup', overturning 'decades' of precedent. In the *Daily Mail*, the decision represented 'a seismic shift in power from the executive to the judiciary'.[25] The Attorney General, Geoffrey Cox QC, commented plaintively that he didn't believe 'any prorogation over the last fifty to hundred years would have survived today's judgment'.[26]

None of that was true. The Supreme Court did no more than remind the executive that parliament must have a say in important decisions. It had not overturned 'decades of precedent' but, rather, complied with legal authority dating back to the seventeenth century. The judgment would not have touched any of the prorogations of the last century because most lasted only a few days. As with most bullshit discourses, however, being 'right' wasn't the point. The government had repositioned itself from villain to victim. The highest court in the land had found that it acted unlawfully, yet the Johnson government and its allies in the press presented it as an innocent victim, stripped of ancient constitutional power by unaccountable judges.[27]

'Appropriated victimhood' is effective because most people have an innate sense of fair play. If someone is oppressed, bullied or victimised, most people would want to see justice done. The rhetoric of victimhood can, therefore, be persuasive in public discourse: 'I have been treated unfairly and now I am owed my due' is a compelling call to action. Unless, of course, the victim is not really a victim and the oppressor is not really an oppressor. Appropriated victimhood works by weaponising our sense of fair play. The powerful adopt the rhetoric of the victim and their actions become justified as a way of setting the scales straight. Their critics and victims are silenced because they are seen as acting unfairly.[28]

We see appropriated victimhood perhaps most blatantly in the debate around 'cancel culture'. Powerful people use their platforms and positions of power to attack vulnerable groups or make racist, sexist or homophobic statements. When others call them out, they claim to have been 'cancelled', their freedom of speech denied (despite still enjoying newspaper columns, TV spots, and many other platforms that their victims and critics are denied). Under 'cancel culture' discourse, the privileged can say whatever they like and those harmed must 'grow a thicker skin', understand the importance of 'hearing things you don't like' in 'constructive debate' or just 'stop being a snowflake'. Anyone who voices disagreement, however, is perpetuating 'cancel culture', 'bullying', and is an enemy of free speech.

Johnson leaned heavily into his appropriated victimhood after the prorogation case. A government found to have acted unlawfully on such a scale might be expected to resign, but it can't be criticised if the judgment was unfair. Moriarty, scornful of the petty constraints of the law, becomes Jean Valjean, persecuted by an unjust system.

## War on History

Eighteen months after the prorogation case the Johnson government began its revenge, introducing legislation to restrict judicial review. The Lord Chancellor, Robert Buckland, claimed that an independent review, led by Lord Faulks, had found:

> A growing tendency for the courts in judicial review cases to edge away from a strictly supervisory jurisdiction, becoming more willing to review the merits of the decisions themselves, instead of the way in which those decisions were made.[29]

In fact, the Faulks Review reached the opposite conclusion, assuring the executive that it could:

be confident that the courts will respect institutional boundaries in exercising their inherent powers to review the legality of
government action. Politicians should, in turn, afford the judiciary the respect which it is undoubtedly due when it exercises
these powers.[30]

The government thus altered the historical record to justify an
attack on those it sees as its political opponents.

Bullshitting about history is possibly the most damaging
form of bullshit because our history determines how we see
ourselves as a society. The *Daily Mail* and the Royal Family work
hard to downplay their associations with the Nazi Party because
that version of their history diminishes the trust and confidence
in which they are held today.[31] All institutions, groups and
individuals create their own versions of history.[32] A hallmark of
autocrats is the imposition of a state-sponsored 'official history'.[33]
The UK is flirting with this very practice.

Governments increasingly use the coercive power of the state
to impose an approved version of British history. One of Michael
Gove's first acts as education secretary, in the early years of the
decade, was to order schools to teach the First World War in a
way that portrayed the UK in a positive light.[34]

Successive governments have promoted an imagined form of
English exceptionalism shaped, in substantial part, by an idea of
our colonial past.[35] It casts Britons as a civilising people. It is
also, inescapably, an identity based on race.[36] The idea of an
innate British superiority survived the decline of empire. It
shines through, for example, in the Brexit discourse. As the
historian Alex von Tunzelmann observed in the *Atlantic*:

It may be easy to overstate a simplistic, literalist connection
between the empire – imagined as glorious, and unjustly lost

– and the impulse to leave the EU. Yet it is hard to avoid the sense that embedded in Brexit is a form of 'Make Britain great again'.[37]

Leading government figures like Boris Johnson and Jacob Rees-Mogg have eulogised the British empire.[38]

This view of English exception is profoundly ahistorical. The British empire was won and maintained by violence, torture and (in at least one instance) genocide.[39] Imagined exceptionalism is just another form of bullshit, albeit set to the mood music of marching redcoats rather than immigration (or antisemitic) hysteria.

The government has used the wartime rhetoric of 'us against them' to justify a campaign to silence any version of history that does not conform to its own. Robert Jenrick promised to save Britain's history, implying that any historian who portrays Britain's past in an unflattering light is attacking Britain itself.[40] Policy Exchange, a think tank allied to the government, runs a 'History Matters' project, which attacks institutions that diverge from the approved version of our past. In 2020, for example, it published a paper attacking Churchill College for holding an event in which academics criticised Winston Churchill.[41] Policy Exchange also maintains a rolling list of those who fail to conform to its chosen view of history.[42]

In the name of 'sav[ing] our history' the government has pressurised the National Trust (an independent charity) to withdraw research exploring the colonial links of its properties, threatened to cut the funding of museums that don't portray colonial figures in a flattering light and coerced schools and universities to remove from the curriculum anything that doesn't fit the government's established view.[43] The author of the National Trust study described being subject to a campaign of harassment as a result of her role:

I've had hundreds of hostile articles written about me, I've had my work misrepresented, I've had threats, I've got police reports, I've had all kinds of problems and attempts to intimidate me at a political level . . . How is that not closing down discussion? How is that not cancel culture?[44]

Reading the government's proposals to 'set right' the Supreme Court's 'error' in the prorogation case, I couldn't help but wonder how long we have before law departments are under pressure to teach the government approved version of the case.

## Bullshit and the Constitution

Bullshit discourses have permeated our understanding of our own constitution. Much of this comes from a single source: the 'Judicial Power Project'. This purports to be a serious study of the constitution, run by Policy Exchange. In practice, it appears more intent on pushing an authoritarian narrative on the basis of misrepresentation. The JPP provided the 'intellectual' basis for several bullshit takes on of the prorogation case. It published a paper claiming the Supreme Court's decision was 'unconstitutional'.[45] The paper (among other basic errors) misrepresented various factual points, failed to engage with most of the constitutional authority after 1689 and suggested that prorogation was governed by a 'constitutional convention' (no such convention exists).

The centrepiece of the JPP's website is a list of '50 problematic cases'. Paul Craig, arguably the UK's pre-eminent constitutional scholar, was unconvinced by the JPP's approach:

Complex judicial decisions are condemned on the basis of a three to five-line summation of the alleged infirmity in the reasoning and result. This comes dangerously close to CNN sound-bite commentary, where there is no warrant for this form of assessment, more especially because the critic can thereby avoid meaningful scrutiny of his or her own reasoning by the very brevity of the summation on the charge sheet.[46]

The JPP's work would unlikely survive the scrutiny of the courtroom or lecture theatre, but it is not intended for either. Its intended audience is politicians, the media and, through them, the public. It doesn't publish in peer-reviewed journals or make reasoned interventions in the cases it later criticises. Instead, it runs a website with digestible articles, holds events for politicians and places articles in friendly media. It has been highly successful. Its events are attended by senior cabinet ministers and its members play a prominent role in public policy.[47] Its ideas may lack intellectual and legal rigour, but the JPP is established in the heart of government.[48]

The JPP claims its main concern is judicial overreach but it seems only to criticise judges who rule against the government.[49] As Thomas Poole, Professor of Law at the LSE and editor of the *Modern Law Journal*, the UK's pre-eminent legal-academic publication, put it:

> its [the JPP's] targets seemingly include any institutional check on executive power. Authoritarian rather than conservative in disposition . . . For all the constitutional posturing, the object of the power so directed is to make it easier to realise a purified version of an imagined past.[50]

Much of the anti-democratic legislation covered in later chapters originated with the JPP. It is particularly effective at dressing up increasingly authoritarian ideas in the guise of democracy.

Judges who force the executive to obey the law or rules that empower parliament or citizens at the expense of the executive are portrayed as frustrating the 'will of the people'. This has distorted the very meaning of democracy. In much of the public's understanding it has been transformed from a network of power sharing to a single majoritarian vote which, once cast, allows the executive to act without constraint.

The danger of bullshit discourse is that reality becomes subjective. As a public, we begin to understand the world by reference to what the powerful tell us it is rather than what it really is. This makes it impossible to faithfully scrutinise them. Bullshit discourse means that 'truth' is not determined by what we can observe before us but by what we can be made to believe. This provides those in power with inordinate influence which threatens the basic tenets of social trust. Public discourse has never been more important because, as we will see in the next chapter, our elected representatives are gradually reduced to the mere *performance* of their democratic duty.

# 3

# ZOMBIE PARLIAMENT

> *... in all the circumstances, the petitioners are reason-*
> *ably apprehensive that the first respondent intends to*
> *continue his course of action of seeking to frustrate the*
> *will and intention of the Union Parliament as*
> *expressed in the 2019 Act.*
>
> O'Neill QC, Welsh, and Fowles,
> *Vince v Advocate General* [2020] S.C. 90

What do we do when the Prime Minister tells his country he will ignore the law? The question may once have belonged in a Chris Mullin novel, yet it happened three times in three years, in 2019, 2020 and 2021.[1] In 2021 the UK found itself in an international court after the executive violated the new treaty with the EU less than three months after signing it.[2] In October 2020, the executive proposed to break a different treaty with the EU, breaching international law, in a 'specific and limited way'.[3] 2019, however, was perhaps the most egregious. The newly elected Johnson government told the country that it would ignore an Act of Parliament, passed just the week before, to avert a no-deal Brexit. In the end, the Court of Session (the highest court in Scotland), in a case brought by businessman Dale Vince, supervised the Johnson government's compliance with the law. I acted for Dale in that case but (as I'm a member of the English, rather than the Scots bar) I wasn't allowed in the courtroom. I ended up taking part in proceedings (mainly via WhatsApp messages to the lawyers in the room) from the bar of the Fairmont Hotel in St Andrews!

The case, which became known as *Vince and others v Lord Advocate*, or 'the Benn Act case', was an example of both parliament and the courts doing exactly what they are supposed to do. Parliament, reflecting the 'will of the people' (the majority of whom did not want a 'no-deal' Brexit[4]), made a law directing the executive to avoid such an outcome. The courts made sure the executive complied with the law. Unfortunately, such constitutional functioning is now the exception rather than the rule. We will look at the government's war on the justice system in the next chapter. In this chapter we will see how parliament itself has been reduced, in many ways, to mere play-acting: the performance of 'a democratic parliament' rather than the real thing. Cambridge University's David Runciman calls this 'zombie democracy'.[5]

## Pretending to be Legislators

The role of MPs is threefold: to make law, hold the executive to account and represent their constituents. The Benn Act showed MPs performing all three. Throughout 2019, MPs repeatedly made it clear to the government that most people opposed a no-deal Brexit. They passed motions, asked questions and lobbied ministers. When ministers refused to rule out a no-deal outcome, parliament passed a law requiring them to do so.

This, however, was exceptional. On leaving parliament in 2015, the veteran Labour MP Frank Dobson said:

> Over the years I've developed a lower and lower appreciation of the place in terms of effectiveness. Our record on passing laws that achieved what it was claimed they would achieve when a minister introduced them [is] absolutely pathetic, quite frankly ... Even if you don't agree with the laws, at least the bloody things ought to work, and so frequently they don't.[6]

Parliament is a place of perverse incentives. MPs receive far greater rewards for appearing to do their job than actually doing it. This conceals the reality that the executive dominates parliament. Thus things mostly work in the opposite way to how they should: the (unelected) executive controls the (elected) legislature.

Parliamentary services like TheyWorkForYou.com record the number of appearances and speeches an MP makes in the chamber of the house. Yet much of this is merely show. Intervening in a debate with a foregone conclusion or attending Prime Minister's Questions to jeer on command contribute relatively little to the actual business of law-making. Effective legislating and scrutinising happen behind the scenes: researching, examining the text of legislation, building coalitions, meeting with constituents and writing to ministers (for example) are all relatively low-profile (and unrewarded) activities. All take considerable amounts of time.

Government business takes precedence in parliament at almost all times, which means that most of the time the executive can, by filling the order paper with various bits of 'business', determine what, when and for how long MPs debate.[7] The government of the day also has almost complete control over the career prospects of most MPs. It determines promotions and demotions, committee positions and public appointments. For most MPs, it is therefore better to agree with (rather than scrutinise) the government. One MP told Isabel Hardman, in an interview for her book *Why We Get the Wrong Politicians*:

> My job on a public bill committee is to assist the minister and get the legislation passed . . . It is a good career move for me as you've got the minister and the whip watching you and it's a real test of your ability to argue for the government.

Another said:

> it was fascinating but frustrating because I ended up agreeing with the [opposition] Labour amendments but couldn't vote for them.[8]

Unsurprisingly, the culture in parliament is not one of dispassionate government but hyper-partisanship. In February 2021, for example, MPs debated the Police, Crime, Sentencing and Courts Bill (of which, more later). This gave the executive new powers to limit free expression and peaceful protest, imprison activists for up to ten years if they 'damage' statues of slave traders and arrest gypsies and travellers on the basis that they might, in future, behave offensively. Given its implications for civil liberties and racist undertones (specifically targeting the traveller minority), one might expect MPs to subject the Bill to serious and forensic consideration. It served, instead, as an example of just how determined MPs are to beat the opposition at any cost. During the debate government backbenchers accused the opposition of defending the 'violent mob' and wanting to allow travellers to 'smash through fences'. In fact, the Bill didn't concern either of those things. Property damage and violent protest unsurprisingly are already criminalised. Government backbenchers were so desperate to show they could beat the opposition that they ended up debating things that weren't actually in the Bill.[9]

Those MPs who attempt to undertake effective scrutiny are deprived of the tools to do so. MPs are only able to employ one or two researchers (and perhaps the same number of constituency staff). The budget for their staff doesn't stretch to a level much beyond a basic graduate salary. People doing an equivalent level of research work in the private sector are generally required to have advanced degrees and substantial experience (and are paid accordingly). MPs have little or no budget to employ outside consultants. When I provide advice to MPs it is always at a vastly reduced rate.

The government, by contrast, has no such disability. While parliamentarians are supported by a staff of twenty lawyers (shared between 650 MPs), ministers benefit from the services of more than 2,000. A former Labour Party researcher recounted to me her experience of the committee stage of the Investigatory Powers Act 2016. She told me how the government ministers and committee members were supported by a large staff of civil servants, all sitting behind them in the committee room. By contrast, she was the only member of staff supporting the opposition members. She wasn't even allowed to sit in the room and ended up sitting in the public gallery and trying to advise by WhatsApp. It is difficult to see how MPs can engage in genuinely effective scrutiny on our behalf when they lack the information and professional support to do so.

MPs are sometimes so badly advised that they do not even know what they are voting on. In December 2020 MPs filed through the lobbies to support a bill giving the government new powers to implement the Brexit withdrawal agreement believing that if they didn't vote with the government:

We leave the transition period without a deal, without a deal on security, on trade, on fisheries, without protection for our manufacturing sector, for farming, for countless British businesses and without a foothold to build a future relationship with the EU.[10]

Those were not the words of an ambitious government backbencher but of the leader of the opposition, former barrister Sir Keir Starmer QC. In fact, voting against the Bill would have had no such consequences. The government doesn't need parliament's consent to ratify or provisionally apply an international treaty (more on that later). MPs were only voting on powers to implement the agreement in domestic law. There are many ways to do this. Parliament could have made specific changes to specific laws to reflect the treaty. Instead, the bill granted the government broad powers to, in effect, overturn any existing law that it considered incompatible with the deal. MPs handed the executive these unprecedented new powers without ever being fully aware of what they were doing.[11]

MPs also lack the powers to conduct serious investigations into government behaviour or policy. While parliament can require ministers to attend to answer questions, ministers often wriggle out of this by sending a deputy. Parliament has no power to compel civil servants or members of the public to answer questions. Even if it did, the structures of parliament do not provide effective fora for questioning. Events like Prime Minister's Questions are rightly criticised as political theatre. Select committees, by contrast, are often held up as examples of high-quality forensic examination. MPs like Margaret Hodge, who chaired the Public Accounts Committee between 2010 and 2015 and engaged in high-profile investigations of tax evasion, are rightly praised for their work. Yet select committees are reliant on the favour of their witnesses. Dominic Cummings, when called before the Digital, Culture, Media and Sport Select Committee, refused to give evidence 'under any circumstances'.[12] Cummings was found 'in contempt of parliament' for his refusal.[13] In theory this can result in a fine or even imprisonment. In practice, however, such a finding is generally meaningless. Just months after being found in contempt, Cummings was appointed to a senior role in government.

When witnesses do attend, they are subjected to questioning that is often anything but forensic. Each member of the select committee is allocated a short period, often no more than a few minutes, to ask their questions. I spend much of my time in court questioning witnesses. Despite what you might see on TV, good cross-examination is rarely dramatic or exciting. It is methodical and meticulous. It requires a lot of preparation and takes a long time. I once questioned a civil servant for nearly two days. This is fairly standard. It often involves returning to the same point repeatedly to tease out the inconsistencies in the witness's story. One company director, over the course of a relatively short cross-examination, gave me three entirely contrasting explanations for the same accounting discrepancy. Barristers don't cross-examine witnesses for fun. We do it because it is the best way to test the strength of a witness's evidence.

Some select committee questioning is excellent, but most do not compare with even the most banal of trials. The level of forensic scrutiny required to properly test a witness is simply not possible in parliament. Ministers and civil servants are rarely, if ever, genuinely pressed. If a select committee becomes too effective at scrutinising the government, it can be disbanded. When the Brexit Select Committee proposed to launch an in-depth investigation into the UK–EU trade agreement, the government abolished it.[14]

It might seem from the above paragraphs that I hold parliamentarians in low regard. Nothing could be further from the truth. I work closely with a number of parliamentarians from all parties and find them to be dedicated, intelligent and selfless. My critique is not aimed at parliamentarians but at the structures which prevent them from doing their jobs. Isabel Hardman asks the question 'why do we get the wrong politicians?' In my view, we don't. Our problem isn't with our politicians but rather our politics. Changing our politicians is unlikely to achieve anything so long as our parliamentary politics remain broken.

## Constitutional Hardball

The government and its supporters reacted to the Benn Act with fury. The Prime Minister lashed out at MPs, accusing them of passing a 'surrender act', conspiring with foreign powers and even committing treason.[15] Why was the government so angry at MPs' disobedience? Perhaps because the executive has become used to its constitutional dominance. The government has always enjoyed significant power over parliament. Until recently, however, there was a convention of constitutional forbearance. This shouldn't be overstated. No government would be happy about its MPs voting with the opposition. The tradition of government whips bullying MPs into line goes back to the days of Edmund Burke.[16] In the past, however, executives have ensured parliament has the opportunity to properly debate important issues, even when doing so created political difficulties. From 1992 to 1993 the Major government set aside nearly a hundred hours of parliamentary time for debate on the

Maastricht treaty. Major knew that the treaty faced substantial opposition from his own party and airing a Conservative civil war in the Commons chamber would be politically embarrassing. He did it anyway.

In the last decade the executive has abandoned traditions of restraint and sought to take full advantage of its dominance over parliament. Levitsky and Ziblatt note this as a common sign of declining democracies:

> 'constitutional hardball': playing by the rules but pushing against their bounds and 'playing for keeps.' It is a form of institutional combat aimed at permanently defeating one's partisan rivals – and not caring whether the democratic game continues.[17]

Over the course of the last decade governments have increasingly used the full extent of their power over the legislature to 'play for keeps'. Early in the decade George Osborne, then Chancellor of the Exchequer, organised a 'treasury support group' of MPs. Junior MPs, keen to curry favour with the Chancellor, were tasked with disrupting opposition members' speeches by heckling, interrupting or simply making so much noise that the speaker could not be heard. This represented a step-change in hyper-partisanship. The Treasury Support Group did not attempt to argue rationally for the government's position; it simply sought to harass and silence anyone who questioned it. Osborne's was by no means the first 'support group' of this kind but it was the largest and most effective.[18]

Governments more and more use their control over parliamentary time and business to stymie debate. In 2012, when four Conservative committee members pushed for amendments to the Overseas Terrorism Compensation Scheme, the government simply had them removed from the committee.[19] In

December 2018 the May government placed its withdrawal agreement with the EU before parliament. The treaty touched on almost every significant area of public policy yet, anticipating opposition, the executive limited debate to just five days. After four days it appeared that the government might lose the vote, so the debate was cancelled.

When by mid-March 2019 it was clear that no consensus could be reached, the government sought an extension to the Brexit deadline (initially for a few days, then to 30 June). It soon became clear that no new agreement would be reached by that date either. The government, however, refused to give MPs time to discuss a solution. The Speaker of the House, John Bercow, allowed MPs to disapply the normal rules and 'take control' of parliamentary business from the executive. Parliament duly passed the EU (Withdrawal) (No. 5) Act 2019 and the EU agreed an extension until 31 October 2019. During the summer Boris Johnson replaced Theresa May as Prime Minister, but by the end of August there were few signs of progress on a revised withdrawal agreement. The Johnson government (again) refused to give MPs time to debate a contingency plan so MPs, once again, voted to take control of the order paper and schedule time to pass the Benn Act.

Unlike its predecessor, the Johnson government wasn't prepared to tolerate this sort of insubordination. The Prime Minister announced that he would 'rather be dead in a ditch' than comply with the Benn Act, so we asked the court to grant an interdict (injunction) forcing him to do so.[20]

The government's position was untenable. Faced with that reality in court it quickly backed down. The Prime Minister's lawyers quickly conceded that he would, in fact, comply with the Act (despite their client and his colleagues making thirty-one separate public statements to the contrary[21]). The Outer

House (the Scots High Court) saw the Prime Minister's concession as sufficient.[22] Dale and the rest of the team, however, were sceptical. Put simply, we didn't trust the Prime Minister's word, even when given in court. So we renewed our claim to the Inner House (the Scots Court of Appeal). The government's lawyers, once again, assured the court that the Prime Minister would, contrary to his public assertions, comply with the Act. The court, however, realised that if it refused our claim, then the Prime Minister would be able to go back on his word and force the UK out of the EU against the wishes of parliament. It therefore took the unprecedented step of 'continuing its consideration' until the letter was sent. In practice this meant that if the Prime Minister failed to seek an extension in time, the court would be on standby to force him to do so. The government, boxed into a corner, sought the Brexit extension on 19 October 2019,[23] and the EU granted the extension the following week.[24]

Outside the courtroom, however, the government sought revenge on the parliamentarians who had stepped out of line. Business Secretary Andrea Leadsom condemned the Speaker for allowing MPs to vote on the Act, calling it a 'flagrant abuse' of the parliamentary process (it's worth remembering that all Bercow had done was allow MP to pass an Act for which there was clearly majority support).[25] Every Conservative MP who had voted for the Benn Act was expelled from the party. At the ensuing general election the Conservative Party announced it would contest the Speaker's seat.[26] This was a breach of convention going back centuries. Bercow, instead, resigned the Speakership and his parliamentary seat.*[27]

---

* It has since emerged that much of Bercow's behaviour 'behind the scenes' was highly problematic.

In December 2019 Bercow was replaced by Sir Lindsay Hoyle. The new Speaker has proved much more compliant. In May 2020 he allowed the government to schedule business so as to exclude more than 200 MPs from parliament. Like most people I'd spent March and April 2020 doing Zoom quizzes and Joe Wicks workouts. But the Speaker's unprecedented decision brought me back into the world of the constitution. One of the excluded MPs asked me to write to the Speaker to remind him that what he had permitted was unlawful.

How did we end up with nearly a third of MPs effectively excluded from parliament (just six months after it had been unlawfully prorogued)?

In April 2020, during the coronavirus pandemic, parliament approved arrangements for MPs to attend debates, announcements and questions, and to vote, remotely using video conferencing technology. The process was approved by a resolution of the house.[28] This was due to expire on 12 May but was subsequently extended until 22 May.

At the height of the pandemic (and its corresponding national lockdown) parliamentary business was relatively sparse. One notable event, however, was Prime Minister's Questions. In the strange silence of an empty House of Commons the new Leader of the Opposition, Sir Keir Starmer QC, took a calm, forensic approach. This began to draw praise even from newspapers, like the *Evening Standard*, which are typically supportive of the government.[29] The Prime Minister, it was commented, looked at sea without the supportive roar from his own benches behind him.[30] The government chose to end the remote parliament arrangements in mid-May, at a time when the country remained firmly in lockdown. While every other profession was advised to work from home, MPs were only allowed to vote if they attended parliament in person. This meant that the substantial number of MPs who were shielding could not vote. The government's own guidance at the time advised people who were shielding not to leave their home. Even for those who were not vulnerable, making the trip to central London at a time of pandemic presented a significant risk.

On 20 May many MPs asked the Leader of the House of Commons, Jacob Rees-Mogg, to extend the remote participation measures. Rees-Mogg refused.[31] Instead, he waited until the measures expired before introducing a new scheme which effectively eliminated remote participation.[32] This meant that MPs who were shielding were barred from voting on the new scheme (then barred, by the new scheme, from voting at all). As many as 250 MPs were excluded from parliament.[33] Rees-Mogg had used the government's control over parliamentary time to ensure that those most likely to vote against his proposals could not vote at all. In doing so he mitigated Johnson's perceived weakness in Prime Minister's Questions. Although some remote participation measures were subsequently reintroduced, these were not of equivalent extent to those in place in April and early May. As Geraint Davies, who was shielding, observed:

> under the new measures I can introduce a bill to the house, but I am not allowed to speak in the house in its favour.

Working with Leigh Day LLP (solicitors) and my colleagues Philip Coppel QC and Estelle Dehon, we wrote to the Speaker and Leader of the House setting out the legal problems with the scheme. Several of those MPs who were still in parliament piled on political pressure.

Rees-Mogg eventually restored remote voting and speaking measures were reintroduced during subsequent lockdowns.*

## Back to the Future

In Chapter 1 we saw how, as the UK constitution evolved, the powers of the state moved from the hands of the executive (in the person of the monarch) to an oligarchy, and then towards democratic control (embodied in parliament). In the last decade that evolution has gone into reverse. Two trends are particularly important. The first is the growing ability of the executive to make law without the consent of parliament. 'Henry VIII clauses' allow the executive to repeal or alter primary legislation without the legislators' permission. They are named after the monarch who, in 1539, gave himself the power to make law without parliament. Even in the nineteenth century, Henry VIII clauses were frowned upon. Between 1888 and 1929 only nine Acts of Parliament contained them.[34] By 1945 they had been 'virtually eradicated'.[35] But, Henry VIII powers began to creep back in from the late 1970s and exploded after Brexit. There are now literally hundreds of such clauses scattered throughout our law.[36] They include the Public Bodies Act 2010, the Data Protection Act 2018, the Withdrawal Agreement Act 2019, the Internal Market Bill 2019–21 and even the Coronavirus Act 2020 and the Divorce, Dissolution and Separation Bill 2019–21. The EU Withdrawal Act 2018 (sometimes called 'The Great Repeal Bill'), intended to allow 'technical' changes after Brexit (such as changing references

---

* In fairness, the government initially robustly rejected the arguments in our letter so we have no way of knowing whether it was our legal argument, political pressure, or something else that caused Rees-Mogg to relent.

to EU regulatory bodies to their UK equivalents), grants the executive Henry VIII powers in almost every area of UK law.

While Henry VIII powers allow ministers to dispense with existing laws, skeleton bills empower the executive to make entirely new law. A skeleton bill is a piece of legislation which, rather than setting down the law, simply gives the executive the power to make law in a particular area.[37] The Agriculture Bill, for example, contained thirty-six clauses, all of which empowered ministers to make law.[38] Ironically, the necessity for skeleton bills is often an indication that the executive is not up to the job of legislating. The Bar Council informed the Lords Constitution Committee that skeleton bills are

> in most cases . . . simply shorthand for [the Government saying] 'we have not thought through what we intend to do'.[39]

The second trend is one of governments using their parliamentary majorities to give their parties an advantage in future elections. In 2013 and again in 2018 governments attempted to redraw the constituency boundaries to their own advantage. In 2021 the Johnson government succeeded. The UK's 'first past the post' electoral system means that the country is split into constituencies. The person who wins the most votes in a constituency becomes that area's MP. In a fair system all constituencies would have roughly the same number of people and be of roughly the same shape. The size and shape of constituencies can, however, be manipulated to give particular parties an advantage. Where I grew up, in Worcestershire, the towns and cities have the largest concentration of people and sometimes these urban constituencies vote Labour. The surrounding countryside has small pockets of Labour support but almost always votes Conservative. While it is, as a whole, a broadly Conservative area, evenly sized and shaped constituencies would likely produce some competition in several seats. Instead, the constituencies are a series of odd shapes, unrelated to geographical features or population centres. The town of Pershore, where I grew up, is tiny. Yet it spans two different constituencies.[40] The effect is to guarantee a Conservative victory in every constituency. The Johnson government boundary changes are estimated to, if people vote the same way as they did in 2019, give Johnson's party an additional ten seats in the next general election.[41]

At the same time the government has made it more difficult for people who don't traditionally vote Conservative to vote at all. The Elections Bill bans people from voting unless they produce photographic ID. It was supposedly introduced to combat 'voter fraud'. In the 2019 general election, just four people were convicted or cautioned for such fraud.[42] By contrast, the government's own research found that 2.1 million voters lack the correct photo ID. The majority of these are from poor or minority backgrounds and these demographics voted disproportionately for opposition parties in 2019.[43] Voter ID laws have been used in the US to disenfranchise millions of poor and minority voters.[44] In 2020 a federal court overturned one such law in North Carolina, saying it disenfranchised black voters 'with almost surgical precision'.[45]

The Johnson government also raised the spending limit for general elections (benefitting the governing party, which tends to attract richer donors than the opposition) and eliminated the Fixed Term Parliament Act 2010. This law set regular dates for elections. With it gone, we have reverted to the old law, whereby the Prime Minister can call a general election at a time most beneficial to his own party.[46]

In all of these examples the government has obtained a majority in parliament. MPs have, in effect, consented to increasing the executive's power at the expense of their own. We, as an electorate, rewarded the Johnson government's assaults on parliament by giving them a majority at the 2019 general election. The *Vince* case shows that MPs still have the power to stand up to the executive: they just choose not to use it. More to the point, we, as electors, consistently choose MPs who will not stand up to the government. We are right to bemoan the inadequacies of our parliamentary system, but we must remember that we are complicit in its failures.

# 4

# JUSTICE DENIED

*The purpose of judicial review is to ensure that the
individual receives fair treatment, and not to ensure
that the authority, after according fair treatment,
reaches on a matter which it is authorised by law to
decide for itself a conclusion which is correct in the
eyes of the court.*

*Lord Hailsham, R. v Chief Constable of North
Wales Ex p. Evans [1982] 1 W.L.R. 1155,
cited in R (NoPI) v Pembrokeshire Coast
National Park Authority (discontinued)*

My first big case was a damp squib. I represented a community
in St Davids, the UK's smallest city, against the local government and a large property developer. The council granted
permission for the developer to build a large budget hotel at the
entry point to the city, dominating the skyline and the area
around it.

St Davids has always been close to my heart. My parents
took my brother and me there on the first holiday I can remember. We stayed in a two-bed cottage by a stream and I thought
it was paradise. Since then, I've spent most summers in and

around St Davids. I learned to surf at the beach and had my first pint in the pub (cider, with my dad, on the day of my GCSE results). Years later I heard that the council may have unlawfully granted planning permission for a major chain to build a new hotel in the city. I offered to assist the local community group campaigning against the development pro bono.

The right of an individual to challenge the government in court is essential to our fourth theme: enfranchisement. If all are equal under the law then we must all be able to enforce our rights in court. The state must accord us all a certain basic standard of treatment and, when it fails to do so, should ensure we can set things straight in court. When the system works properly, the courts treat secretaries of state and millionaires the same as the poor and unemployed. Unfortunately, in practice, it doesn't always work out this way.

St Davids is more of a village than a city. It has a square, a couple of pubs and a cathedral. Many people work in locally owned hospitality businesses; mainly restaurants, cafes and B&Bs. The developer's proposal was for a sixty-three-bed budget hotel. This would, by economies of scale, easily undercut the locally owned alternatives. It doesn't take much to realise that the proposal would be catastrophic for the local economy. The developers, however, produced an economic assessment indicating a net economic gain. The community members were, unsurprisingly, suspicious. They asked three leading economists, from the universities of Oxford, Cambridge and Cardiff, to prepare independent reports. Predictably these all showed that the hotel would likely cause local businesses to fold and unemployment to rise. The council, however, accepted the developer's economic assessment almost without question and ignored the experts put forward by my clients.

Planning law comes in two tiers. At the top are the planning acts. These set out the structure of the planning system, who takes what decisions and how these decisions must be made. They also give the Westminster and devolved governments the power to set national planning policy, and local governments powers to set local planning policy. The second tier is planning policy. National policy sets out the broad objectives for the planning system, such as the sort of development to be encouraged and the general principles that should be taken into account when deciding whether to grant planning permission. Local planning policy is determined by local authorities and sets out the specific criteria for planning permission in the local area. Planning decisions are made, in the first instance, by local authorities, applying local and national policy within the framework set out by the planning acts. We will explore how planning policy and decisions are made in more detail in a later chapter. For now, it suffices to say that while the courts cannot interfere in the substance of planning decisions, much of planning law concerns questions of whether decision-makers took the right information into account and analysed it in the right way.

St Davids was such a case. The correct approach to economic assessments was set out in the national planning policy for Wales. That policy, at the time, included a specific instruction that decision-makers must ensure that they rely on 'robust' economic evidence. The local authority in St Davids had not, in my view, relied on 'robust' economic evidence. Indeed, our analysis suggested they had done quite the opposite. Even if I was wrong on that point, I argued, there is a general rule in public law that decision-makers must take into account all material considerations and discard all immaterial considerations. The alleged flaws in the developer's economic assessment were material considerations. The local authority was, I suggested, not entitled to base its decision on the developer's economic report. It wasn't necessarily a 'slam dunk' case, but it was certainly a decent point to argue. I put it together with a number of other grounds and we were ready to seek a judicial review.

## Justice and Democracy

The justice system has many roles. It ensures that the laws made by parliament are enforced, disputes between citizens are arbitrated impartially and the executive obeys the law. The latter process is known as 'judicial review' and is perhaps the justice system's most important constitutional role. Our democracy is only as strong as its laws. If the government isn't forced to obey the law then it can ride roughshod over our rights. But it's not enough just to say that the government must obey the law; sometimes governments have to be forced to do so. Laws that cannot be enforced in practice are just a waste of the draftsman's ink. Rights that cannot be vindicated are no more than daydreams.

The justice system is comprised of the 'judiciary' (judges) and all of the institutions and systems that enable them to do their job. This includes the court estate, court staff and the systems and initiatives that make them accessible to the public, such as legal aid.

The judiciary has a 'private' role and a 'public' role. In its private role, it determines disputes about the law between private individuals and companies, including claims like breach of contract, personal injury and divorce. In its public role, it determines disputes between individuals and the state. These include criminal cases (i.e. the state claims that an individual has committed a crime) and 'public law' cases. 'Public law' is the law of government power. It lays down the powers that the executive can exercise and the limits on those powers. Public law is litigated through judicial review.

Judicial review cases are never about whether a decision is 'right but, rather, whether it was made in the right way'. Government decisions will almost always be contested. The courts, however, do not get involved in questions of public policy. Rather, their role is to ensure that whatever decision the government takes is within the boundaries set by the law. This means within the scope of the government's legal powers and in accordance with the law of fairness, rationality and human rights. As Lord Justice Hickinbottom reminded both sides in another case in which I was (briefly) involved:

> The subject matter raises passions on both sides. However, consideration of this claim must be focused exclusively on the question of whether the Respondent [the government] has acted in accordance with the law. The courts are not concerned at all with the merits of leaving or remaining in the EU.[1]

The judiciary is essential for three reasons. First, it upholds the principle of parliamentary sovereignty by ensuring that everyone (including the executive) obeys the laws passed by parliament. As Lord Dyson (a former Supreme Court judge) put it:

> [The role of the judiciary] includes ensuring that these bodies comply with their statutory obligations. Since these obligations are the result of the democratic process, their enforcement is an essential handmaiden to democracy itself . . . It is true that the interpretation of statutes is undertaken by judges and, as we are frequently reminded, judges in the UK at any rate are not elected by the people and are not accountable to Parliament. But that should not be a cause for concern, since the aim of the interpretative process undertaken by the judges is to ascertain and give

effect to the will of Parliament . . . Insisting on the performance of these obligations is one of the hallmarks of any truly democratic system.[2]

Second, the judiciary ensures that the executive does not abuse its authority. Our constitution and laws give the government extraordinarily broad powers. It can, for example, dismiss parliament, arrest individuals it considers a threat and even (as we learned throughout 2020 and 2021) close down entire sections of the country. The executive controls the civil service, police, security services and the army and has a budget of over £900 billion.[3]

In 1887 the great historian Lord Acton wrote a letter to his friend Bishop Creighton discussing the dangers of excessive government power. He compared the UK's emerging democratic constitution favourably to states like Prussia, in which power was concentrated in the hands of the monarch. He warned that where power is not constrained by checks and balances it will almost inevitably abused. The letter is famous for the phrase:

power tends to corrupt, and absolute power corrupts absolutely.[4]

Lord Acton's aphorism is often quoted as a sort of doom-laden prophecy. But it's really a warning about the risks of power above the law. Unless the ruler is accountable to the law, there is no incentive for the ruler to act lawfully. Where the ruler acts unlawfully, i.e. outwith the constraints approved by, and necessary to, the democratic process, democracy falters. Lord Acton's central thesis remains as true today as ever.

The primary check on the abuse of executive power is parliament. But parliament is not always capable of providing the necessary protection. There is both a principled and an institutional reason for this. From a principled perspective, parliament represents the majority. But the rights of the minority must also be protected. The reason for this is simple: the majority must be able to change. A majority acting with unchecked power could make itself the majority in perpetuity by removing the rights of its political opponents.

Where the executive commands a majority in parliament, MPs have no incentive to remedy the illegal act. The courts, however, have no interest in who happens to control the majority in parliament at any given time. They apply the law, whoever is in government. This is essential to both the day-to-day functioning and the very essence of our constitution.

From an institutional perspective, parliament cannot perform the same role. The executive's dominance of parliament was discussed in the last chapter. An executive seeking to avoid accountability for an illegal act could simply prevent parliament from considering it. Even if the executive left parliament alone, the government performs so many complex tasks every day that it would be impossible for parliament to consider every single alleged breach of the law. Further, parliament is a partisan institution. MPs vote, at least in part, based on party loyalty. It's hardly an atmosphere conducive to forensic and dispassionate consideration of the facts of a case (and it's arguably not supposed to be).

Judicial review fills this chink in the constitutional armour and ensures that individual rights are protected from abuse.[5]

The judiciary gives effect to the equality principle by enforcing civil rights. These include freedom of expression, the right to be treated fairly (including the right to a fair hearing), freedom from torture or cruel or degrading treatment and the right to privacy. Some of these rights are enshrined in statute but many have their roots in the common law. Many civil rights are included in the European Convention on Human Rights. Those who criticise human rights as 'foreign' impositions tend to forget that the convention was drafted by British lawyers, on the instructions of the (then) Prime Minister, Winston Churchill, and the rights it protects are based on the rights enshrined for centuries in the common law.[6]

The third purpose of the judiciary is to uphold the rule of law. This combines the principles embodied in the first two purposes with a third element: fairness. It means the same rules apply to everyone, whether prince or beggar. The rule of law is also a constraint upon judicial review: the courts, like the executive, are not entitled to (and do not) apply one rule for their friends and another for their foes. Similarly, the courtroom is (in theory) one of the few places the government can't dominate its opponents. Outside the courtroom the government wields the vast power of state. Inside the courtroom, it should be just another party (although, as we will see in later chapters, it's not always treated like this).

Since the early years of the twentieth century the number of judicial review claims has increased substantially. There are three reasons for this. The first was discussed in Chapter 1: as the UK became a more democratic state over the course of the twentieth century, the courts increasingly forced the government to comply with the law. The increase in the number of judicial review cases over the last hundred years reflects the fact that the executive is now more accountable for its actions.

Second, the volume and complexity of legislation has increased substantially over the last hundred years. While the number of Acts of Parliament declined between 1900 and 2019 (from well over a hundred per annum in the early years of the last century to just thirty-three in 2019), the Acts passed have become substantially longer. More importantly, there has been a corresponding rise in secondary legislation. As Isabel Hardman reports:

> Research by the Hansard Society found that between 1950 and 1990, the number of statutory instruments produced each year was rarely higher than 2,500. From 1992, it has never dipped below 3,000. And Parliament only scrutinises on average 1,200 of those regulations.[7]

Primary legislation (which is made by parliament) is immune from judicial review. Public law claims therefore only consider primary legislation when examining whether the executive has acted within the powers granted by parliament. Secondary legislation, on the other hand, is made by the executive under powers granted (by parliament) in primary legislation. This means that, where it is contained in secondary legislation, the law itself can be challenged.[8] Where, for example, secondary legislation forces government bodies to act in a way that is discriminatory, the courts may strike it down. The increase in the volume of secondary legislation therefore means that there is a substantially larger body of law that is amenable to judicial review.

Finally, it is worth pointing out that before 1983 public law claims did not have to be brought by judicial review.[9] As a result, we don't really know how often the government was challenged in court before that time because there are no accurate records. Given these three factors, an expansion in the volume of judicial review is, over the course of the last century, to be expected.

The number of claims has, however, been essentially static since the beginning of the twenty-first century. Indeed, there were fewer claims made in 2019 than 2000.[10] Around 50% of all claims are settled (often to the benefit of the claimant). The ultimate success rate for judicial review claims has remained somewhere between 40% and 50% throughout the century.[11] This is broadly equivalent to the success rate for private law claims.[12]

The judiciary has been criticised for 'interfering in politics'. It's not clear what this means. It is certainly true that the judiciary sometimes makes decisions that are embarrassing for the government. This is to be expected; any government would (rightly) be embarrassed if a court found it had acted unlawfully. None of the supposedly 'political' decisions, however, involved courts interfering with or altering public policy. Rather, the courts limit themselves to determining whether the government has abused its powers or acted outside the law.

The first Miller case, for example, was criticised because the courts allegedly 'interfered' in a 'political' decision. The alleged 'political decision' was whether the UK should, in accordance with the result of the 2016 Brexit referendum, send a letter to the EU, pursuant to Article 50 of the Treaty on European Union, triggering the beginning of the Brexit process. But the court didn't actually express any view on whether or not the UK should send such a letter. Indeed, both the High Court and, on appeal, the Supreme Court explicitly stated that the decision whether or not to send the letter was none of the court's business. Both courts, however, determined that it must be parliament (i.e. the elected representatives of the people) which decided whether or not to send the letter rather than the government. In other words, the court was not concerned with what decision should be made but, rather, who should make the decision.

The court's reasoning was that beginning the process of Brexit would inevitably mean that certain laws made by parliament would be changed or eliminated. The court followed the ancient legal principle that where parliament makes a law only parliament can 'unmake' that law. Thus, while the judgment undoubtedly embarrassed the May government, it wasn't because the court interfered in politics. The irony, of course, is that parliament was perfectly happy to send the Article 50 letter (and this should have been obvious, given that all the main parties explicitly supported starting the Brexit process). Indeed, the May government only had itself to blame for its humiliation. Had it not tried to (completely unnecessarily) usurp powers reserved for the elected parliament, the courts would never have had to set it right.

As two separate independent inquiries have recently confirmed, the judiciary generally does its constitutional job and stays within its constitutional lane.[13] That job, however, is becoming much harder in the face of attacks from both the government and parliament.

## War on Justice

Judicial review is, by its very nature, inconvenient for the executive. It inevitably can make life awkward for ministers and local government. In St Davids we were asking the court to tell the local authority that it had done its job badly.

This tension between the executive and the judiciary is the very purpose of the constitution, not a glitch. For centuries executives have accepted this tension and even welcomed the oversight of the courts as a means to ensure better government. As the civil service guidance on judicial review reminds officials:

Administrative law (and its practical procedures) play an important part in securing good administration, by providing a powerful method of ensuring that the improper exercise of power can be checked.[14]

Planning challenges, like St Davids, are a case in point: decision-makers often look to previous, similar, cases for instruction on how they should go about determining a planning application. Not all ministers take this view. The courts are increasingly seen by the executive as a rival for political power. This recalls Levitsky and Ziblatt's description of autocrats who seek to hide their repression behind a 'veneer of legality'. They seek either to 'capture' or 'eliminate' the 'referees'. Modern European autocrats like Viktor Orbán in Hungary and Andrzej Duda in Poland both began their journey to autocracy by delegitimising the courts in the eyes of the public then either packing them with loyalists or replacing them with more pliable institutions.[15]

Some ministers have attempted to interfere directly in the justice system by pressuring judges to rule in their favour. In 2003 David Blunkett (then Home Secretary), after a number of defeats in court, invited the Lord Chief Justice to a private dinner so they could 'run through the issues informally and quietly'.[16] In April 2020 the Home Office wrote to the President of the Immigration Tribunal to complain about the 'level of grants of bail in recent weeks'. The judge, in his response, felt compelled to remind the Home Secretary that 'as independent judiciary we decide bail applications in accordance with the law'.[17] In other words: the Home Office should not be attempting to pressure judges to decide more cases in its favour.

When direct attempts to exert influence don't work, governments and their media allies have waged a campaign to delegitimise the justice system. The executive's attacks on the courts have built slowly for many years. In the early 1990s Michael Howard, then Home Secretary, used a radio interview to attack a judge who had ruled against him in a terrorism case. Ten years later, Howard's successor, David Blunkett, attacked judges for not living in the 'real world' and upholding 'airy-fairy civil liberties'. Fellow ministers anonymously briefed the press that judges who passed insufficiently tough sentences were 'muddled and confused old codgers'.[18]

Ironically, after criticising judges who enforced the human and civil rights of the immigrants he unlawfully tried to deport, Blunkett was forced to resign when he was accused of fast-tracking the immigration application of his lover's nanny.[19] He then took a job writing columns for the *Sun*, which included the headlines: 'Our justice system is a sick joke', 'Give that judge a brain transplant', and 'Bewigged menaces who make the law look like an ass'.[20]

Before 2010, cabinet members pushed back when their colleagues attacked the judiciary. Lord Falconer (then Lord Chancellor), for example, appeared on *Question Time* to defend a junior judge after his cabinet colleague John Reid criticised a prison sentence as 'unduly lenient'. When a justice minister, Vera Baird MP, criticised a judge on the *Today* programme, Falconer forced her to apologise.[21]

Since 2010, however, ministers have attacked the judiciary with impunity. When Theresa May, then Home Secretary, saw a deportation order overturned (because May failed to follow her own official guidance) she made the bullshit claim that she had lost the case because the man's 'human rights' made it unlawful for him to leave his cat.[22] In 2013 May told parliament: 'Some judges have . . . chosen to ignore the will of parliament and go on putting the law on the side of foreign criminals instead of the public.'[23] This was also bullshit. The 'will of parliament' is expressed by Acts of Parliament. Judges cannot overturn or rule contrary to an Act of Parliament. May had accused the judiciary of an offence that it was impossible for them to commit. She, nevertheless, returned to the theme in her speech to the Conservative Party conference in 2016, drawing a standing ovation for her condemnation of 'activist left-wing human rights lawyers'.[24]

*Miller I* unleashed a new level of invective. In that case the court did no more than remind the government that it could not make new laws without an Act of Parliament.[25] Yet Dominic Raab railed against 'An unholy alliance of diehard Remain campaigners, a fund manager [and] an unelected judiciary' which must not 'thwart the wishes of the British public'.[26] A year later the Home Office accused 'activist lawyers' of frustrating attempts to deport 'illegal immigrants'.[27] In fact, the deportations in question had failed due to the Home Office's own errors.[28] Nevertheless, the Home Secretary doubled down, condemning 'activist lawyers' in a follow-up tweet and again in her speech to the 2020 Conservative Party conference.[29] After closing almost a third of all courts in England and Wales since 2010, the Prime Minister blamed the resulting backlog of cases on 'lefty human rights lawyers'.[30]

The government's media allies often ape the language of authoritarian regimes. Headlines like 'Enemies of the People', 'Judges vs the People' and 'After judges block Brexit your country really needs you' (ending with the line 'Rise up people of Britain and fight, fight, fight') frame enforcing the law as an attack on the nation as a whole.[31] After *Miller II/Cherry*, Quentin Letts accused Lady Hale of 'corruption' because she would be taking up an unpaid post at Oxford when she retired from the Bench. He called judges 'fair game' and demanded their spouses be interrogated for their voting history.[32] The *Sun* regularly 'names and shames' judges whom it perceives as insufficiently compliant with its views.[33] Judges and lawyers are now often threatened or physically attacked.[34] More than two-thirds of judges in England and Wales feel less well respected than they were five years ago and fewer than 10% feel valued by the government (and only 12% by the media).[35]

## Legislating for Impunity

Our biggest problem in the St Davids case was not legal argument but the procedural hurdles thrown up by successive governments that made it harder for citizens to challenge authorities in court. In 2012 the Cameron government, embarrassed by its failure to deport the extremist preacher Abu Qatada, restricted citizens' right to judicial review.[36] In respect of planning cases, it halved the time limit for bringing cases, increased the fees that must be paid before a claim can be issued and restricted the right to an oral hearing. This meant my St Davids clients had to rush their initial grounds of challenge and pay a substantial fee (more than they could afford) just to bring the case; and even then they were not guaranteed a genuine opportunity to present their case to a judge.

Cameron claimed his reforms were necessary to reduce delays in the justice system. If that was their real purpose they didn't work. The time taken from the start of a claim to a final verdict remains broadly the same as it was in 2012 and the backlog of cases waiting to be heard has increased.[37] The real impact of Cameron's reforms was to make it harder for people like my clients in St Davids to bring claims. A claimant with plenty of money can pay for a large enough team of barristers and solicitors to investigate, draft and issue a claim in the six weeks available. This is much more difficult when all you can afford is a single junior barrister working alone without payment. When combined with the increase in the fee charged just to submit a claim for judicial review (which has jumped from around £60 to £770 over the course of the last decade[38]), the Cameron reforms exclude ordinary people from judicial review while leaving the way open to those with sufficient financial resources.

In 2020 the Johnson government extended the executive's legal impunity, passing legislation restricting claims for war crimes and negligence by the MoD. The government claimed that the UK's armed forces were facing defeat not by enemy action but 'judicial diktat'.[39] I was sceptical and so suggested Geraint Davies ask the Lord Chancellor in parliament about the evidential basis for his claims:

Davies: 'Can the Justice Secretary give an example of a military operational decision that has been changed as a result of court action or the threat of court action, and an example of a vexatious claim that has not been dismissed by the courts, with costs?'

Buckland: 'I take it that the hon. Gentleman is referring to the Bill that will be debated this afternoon, which contains important provisions to get the balance right between the need to make sure that our armed services are supported properly and their contribution is valued and the need to make sure that, like everybody else, no one is above the law. There have at times in years gone by been a number of examples where members of our gallant armed services have been unfairly exposed to the potential of legal action, which has caused real hurt, disquiet and genuine concern among the general public. It is right that in the Overseas Operations (Service Personnel and Veterans) Bill we take corrective action to get that balance more finely adjusted.'[40]

In other words: no. The Secretary of State, despite referring to 'a number of examples', could not name a single one. This wasn't a surprise; none existed. The effect of the legislation is to immunise the government from genuine claims brought by service personnel and the victims of war crimes.[41]

Parliament has increasingly legislated to prevent the law from applying to the government or its allies. The legislation providing for the Brexit referendum disapplied many of the penalties for breaching electoral law. In a normal election, violating campaign spending limits can lead to the result being overturned. When Vote Leave was found to have broken electoral law, it could only be punished by a (comparatively small) fine.[42] While I was writing this book parliament passed legislation banning citizens from suing the government if it broke the law in relation to various parts of the Brexit withdrawal agreement, and allowing ministers and officials to confer immunity on agents who commit crimes against its political opponents (including murder and torture).[43]

Parliament is currently considering a bill to further restrict the right to judicial review.[44]

## Access to Justice

I prepared much of the St Davids case sitting with my laptop at a corner table in the same pub I visited in my youth. All litigation is a risk, but I was confident that we had a case worth arguing. I was ready to go to court.

But my clients never got to challenge the council's decision. This wasn't because we had a bad case, or because they changed their minds about its lawfulness. It wasn't even because a judge ruled against us. It was because they couldn't afford it. Although I was working for free, my clients still had to pay the large court fee imposed by the Cameron government. If we lost, they would have been forced to pay the other side's costs. We knew these already amounted to thousands, possibly tens of thousands, of pounds.[45] My clients were mostly minimum wage workers. Even with free representation, they simply couldn't afford to bring the case. So they didn't. They're not the only ones. Successive governments have priced most people out of judicial review. Something Tom Hickman QC calls 'public law's disgrace'.[46]

More than half a century ago, Attlee's cabinet came up with a solution to the affordability issue: legal aid. The aim was to ensure:

> no one would be financially unable to prosecute a just and reasonable claim or defend a legal right; and to allow counsel and solicitors to be remunerated for their services.[47]

In other words, if the courts provide a level playing field, legal aid ensures everyone can get on the pitch.

When the Legal Aid Act 1949 was passed it covered 80% of the population. This may seem high, but litigation is expensive. Barristers and solicitors must train for at least six years. At my set, we rarely take pupils unless they have at least a decade of combined higher education and work experience. In 2017 there were 15,518 applications for just 224 pupillage vacancies.[48] Accordingly, both solicitors and barristers command substantial fees. My income as a barrister probably puts me in the top 10% of earners, but I certainly couldn't afford to bring a judicial review. When I was hit by a car a few years ago, the only way I could afford the legal bills was to find a firm willing to act on a 'no win no fee' basis. If everyone is to have access to the highest quality legal advice and representation, then most people will need help. As the issues we faced became more complex, working out our rights and disputes in court became more challenging, and, accordingly, the legal aid bill increased.

The Thatcher government began to discuss rolling back legal aid in the 1980s, but the Cameron coalition was the first to impose real cuts. It justified its policy by warning of 'fat cat lawyers' who were 'getting rich off legal aid'. Lurid stories about the salaries earned by lawyers populated the tabloids.[49] Much of this was misleading. Many legal aid lawyers earned less than the minimum wage.[50] But let's, for argument's sake, take the claim at face value and imagine all lawyers earn high salaries. The law is a highly specialist and technical discipline. The best lawyers command high salaries because their skills are in demand. Those who fail to reach the required level of excellence tend to leave the profession. If legal aid does not pay the same rates that lawyers can earn by taking on private cases, then many lawyers simply won't do legal aid work. Why should they? Should someone who has trained for ten years accept less than they are worth just because legal aid, rather than a private client, is paying? Many of us, of course, do exactly that. I devote about a third of my time to working pro bono on cases like St Davids. So the justice system relies on the personal ad hoc decision of lawyers choosing to occasionally volunteer.

The Cameron government removed legal aid for 80% of those eligible. Nearly a fifth of specialist legal aid law firms closed over the following decade.[51] Ministers justified the cuts as necessary to stop 'nuisance suits' and balance the budget but, in private, admitted that the reforms were driven by the need to 'pass the Daily Mail test'.[52]

Some of the most vicious cuts were reserved for judicial review. Legal aid is now restricted, in judicial review cases, to those receiving means-tested benefits. If a claimant has savings, then they are generally ineligible for legal aid. This means that some of my clients in St Davids would have been required to choose between enforcing their rights against the government and owning a house or paying for their retirement. It is a societal fiasco. The effect is that challenging the government in court has become a privilege rather than a right.

It's not surprising that ever more lawyers are either leaving, or choosing not to join, the legal aid sector. I was one of the latter. My friend Jane (not her real name), however, went to work for a small legal aid firm straight out of law school. Jane works sixty to eighty hours most weeks and is paid for about half of that time. Most weeks she earns less than the minimum wage. Nevertheless, when we met for a walk in Battersea Park (to talk about this book), she still insisted on buying the coffees. Like many firms across the country, Jane's is cutting back on its legal aid work. The rates have been cut so low, and so few people are eligible, that firms can't break even unless they take on ever larger amounts of private sector work to cover their losses from legal aid. Good lawyers, who joined the firm at the same time as Jane, are leaving. Many are unable to justify the all-consuming hours and low pay as they begin to start families. As a result, the legal sector is beginning to see 'advice deserts'; whole areas of law in which specialist advice is impossible to find because no one can afford to do that sort of work any more.[53]

The justice system is now a class system. We are divided between those who can afford proper legal representation and can therefore access the level playing field of the courts and those who cannot. Many people now represent themselves in court, or else turn to untrained, low-cost alternatives.[54] Litigants in person start with an enormous disadvantage when arguing against trained counsel. My chambers has fifty-eight members and I have not once heard of any of my colleagues losing to a litigant in person. Non-specialist advocates are little better.

When I appeared against one such advocate (who was at least ten years my senior), I had to explain to him how and when to address the judge.

The justice system is often portrayed as a realm of pompous, berobed lawyers and judges, but these optics are beside the point. The justice system's *raison d'être* is to ensure that individual citizens in this country can enforce their legal rights. The right to justice is a right to have rights. Over the last decade governments have slowly stripped citizens of the right to have rights, allowing the powerful to act with impunity. Acts of Parliament become no more than polite suggestions. Civil rights are reduced to aspirations.

As with so many other attacks on our constitution we citizens have allowed this to happen. Just as we rewarded Cameron's attacks on the justice system with a majority in 2015, we rewarded Johnson's attack on parliament with a majority in 2019. Of course, very few people took the justice system into account when casting their vote in the 2015 general election. But perhaps they should have. Constitutional rights are the most important thing we have because it is only by protecting our democracy that we can preserve and achieve everything else that is important to us in the political realm. We can never afford to take our foot off the constitutional pedal, not least because while the executive spent the last decade taking rights away from citizens, it was also consolidating its own powers.

# 5

# TOO MUCH GOVERNMENT

*It is difficult to see how a reasonable prime minister,
properly advised, could adopt the position that the
view of officers who are not security specialists should
outweigh the view of the security services about what
disclosures are prejudicial to the security services.*
*From my advice in The R(Bureau of Investigative
Journalists) v The Prime Minister (not issued)*

One of the best things about being a barrister is that you might
get to solve people's problems. When I represent an abused
spouse, I may not be able to resolve all of her troubles, but I can,
(if only a little) empower her against her abuser. Few moments
in court are more satisfying than when, often about halfway
through cross-examination, an abusive spouse realises that
(perhaps for the first time ever) they are about to be held responsible for their actions.

It is, by this same token, incredibly frustrating when the law
can't fix a problem. In constitutional law, it happens all too often.
Many of the 'rules' we expect government to observe are not
'laws' but rather informal codes of behaviour. Some of these are
given specific names (like the constitutional conventions) while

others are simply expectations. Much of the non-legal area of the constitution is not enforced by the courts, but by political pressure. Parliament can exert pressure by passing motions or even Acts. Given, however, the dominance of the executive over parliament, this is relatively rare. More often political pressure is exerted informally, by a combination of MPs and civil society. This can be through questions, statements in parliament, discussions behind the scenes and debates in the press, on television and within social media, or even by utilising the perceived 'mood' of the country.

Informal or 'unwritten' rules offer ways for parliament and citizens to control the executive, but what happens when the government just doesn't care? As discussed in Chapter 2, our national discourse bears increasingly little relation to reality. It's difficult to hold the government to account when you don't know what's true. If the executive chooses, it can just ignore the non-legal rules of the constitution and, unless MPs step up, there's very little anyone can do about it.

I learned this lesson the hard way during a case in November 2019. It was officially called *The Bureau of Investigative Journalists v The Prime Minister*, but I remember it as 'the Russia Report case'. This was a case in which the Johnson government broke a number of unwritten rules, all falling under the same overarching principle: the executive should not let political considerations influence national security decisions. This chapter is about that case; what happens when an executive decides it doesn't want to observe the unwritten rules of the constitution, which usually pertain to ethics in some way or another. It speaks to our third theme: centralisation – how power is becoming increasingly concentrated in the hands of the executive and its allies.

## The Russia Report Case

To understand the Russia Report case, one must first understand parliament's Intelligence and Security Committee (the ISC). The position of the intelligence and security services in a democratic state involves a tricky balance. On the one hand unaccountable institutions with power to spy on, imprison and sometimes even kill other people are inherently problematic. On the other, our security services are necessary to protect us. Too much transparency would make it rather difficult for them to do an effective job. One of the ways in which we balance these two competing imperatives is the ISC.

The ISC is a committee of MPs and peers tasked with oversight of the security services. It is comprised of parliamentarians who have been security vetted and so are entitled to see secret information. This means that the security services (which include MI5 and MI6 as well as various other government agencies) must answer to elected representatives; but the resultant risk to national security is minimal. As one might expect, the ISC is very careful about how its reports are published. In theory, it seeks to publish as much information as possible without compromising national security. The Justice and Security Act 2013 requires the ISC to work with the Prime Minister to ensure that appropriate information is redacted. In practice this means that the committee works with the security services and Cabinet Office security staff to agree redactions and the Prime Minister signs off on the result.

In 2017, then Prime Minister Theresa May used a speech in the City of London to deliver a warning. Russia, she said, was:

> seeking to weaponise information. Deploying its state-run
> media organisations to plant fake stories and photo-shopped

images in an attempt to sow discord in the west and undermine our institutions.[1]

In a follow-up briefing, Downing Street staff said the speech was based on a 'growing body of evidence' that Russia was attempting to interfere in the politics and elections of Western states, including the UK.[2]

In the wake of May's speech, the ISC began an investigation into the allegations. It heard evidence from the UK's intelligence agencies as well as third party experts. By March 2019 the committee had completed its report. It then began working with the security services and agencies to decide which parts would be redacted and which would be published. By October 2019 they had reached an agreement and on 17 October 2019 the report was sent to the Prime Minister.

But there it stayed.[3]

By the start of November MPs were beginning to wonder when the report would be published. The Prime Minister's spokesperson initially told journalists that the report was still being vetted. Representatives of the security services themselves revealed this to be a lie. A source told the *Independent*:

> We are as much spectators in this as you are. All the redactions necessary have been done and no last-minute issues have arisen. We have no objections to the report being published now.[4]

Both the Commons and the Lords were beginning to lose patience. Christopher Pincher, then Minister for Europe and the Americas (in the Commons) and Lord Ahmad, then Minister of State at the Foreign and Commonwealth Office (in the Lords), told parliament that the Prime Minister usually takes at least six weeks to scrutinise ISC reports and the Russia Report was being considered by 'senior officials' in the Cabinet Office.[5] The Chairman of the ISC, Dominic Grieve QC, contradicted Pincher. He told the Commons that consideration by the Prime Minister himself normally takes no more than ten working days and the report had been approved for publication by the Cabinet Office before 17 October 2019.[6] Pincher and Ahmad's statements were bullshit.

Grieve's intervention made no difference and parliament ran out of time. On 6 November 2019 it was dissolved in preparation for a general election. The Prime Minister had broken the unwritten rule that ISC reports are released once they are cleared by the security services. This meant that the UK would hold a general election without knowing the extent to which foreign powers were interfering in it.

The Bureau of Investigative Journalists wasn't prepared to let that slide. They instructed solicitors Rosa Curling and Erin Alcock of Leigh Day to challenge Johnson in court. Rosa and Erin pulled together a bumper team of barristers including Victoria Wakefield QC and Malcolm Birdling of Brick Court, Julianne Morrison of Monkton Chambers and (mainly carrying the bags) me.

The Freedom of Information Act 2000 (which we will discuss in more detail in the next chapter) provides a statutory scheme for the disclosure of information. But it takes a long time. Our goal, in the Russia Report case, was to force publication of the report in time for the general election. I suggested that we eschew the 2000 Act and rely, instead, on an older common law principle by which public bodies must actively publish information where it is in the public interest to do so.[7] Given the Prime Minister was holding information that could reveal whether Russia was interfering in the election that was currently ongoing, I thought we had an arguable case. The others agreed and we got to work.

## The Will of the People

Our case relied on convincing the court that the public interest in disclosing the report (i.e. alerting the public to possible interference in the election) was greater than the public interest in keeping it a secret. Part of a junior barrister's role is to try to work out what the other side will say. As I started my research, I realised that, at some point in the last decade, the government's rhetoric had changed. Ministers were implying that the executive, not parliament, embodies the 'will of the people'.

This is about more than mere words. It is an attempt to shift the constitutional balance of power. The executive does not, in reality, represent the 'will of the people' because the executive isn't elected. By pretending that it does, the government is able to concentrate real power away from democratically elected representatives and into the hands of a small (largely unelected) group.

In 2018, MPs voted to order the government to disclose the Attorney General's legal advice on the effect of the 'Northern Ireland backstop'. The government refused. The Attorney General told the house:

> A Minister is obliged to have regard to the public interest and
> the national interest. Let us suppose I had given any such advice
> that has been requested by the right hon. and learned Member
> for Holborn and St Pancras (Keir Starmer), and let us suppose
> that that advice had covered all sorts of matters, including our
> relationships with foreign states and including arguments that
> might be deployed in the future – and their strengths and

weaknesses – and including matters of acute importance to this country; would it be right for the Attorney General, regardless of the harm to the public interest, to divulge his opinion? I say to the right hon. and learned Lady that it would not.[8]

Cox's words were nonsensical. How can you act 'in the national interest' by refusing the instruction of the nation's elected representatives? Cox's words make perfect sense, however, if you believe that the 'will of the people' is no longer expressed in the people's choice of legislature but rather in the arbitrary decisions of the (unelected) executive.

After winning the election in 2019 Johnson doubled down on this rhetoric, claiming that he would lead 'the people's government'. This perspective elevates the executive above the other branches of the state. The government has become the embodiment of the national will, rising above such petty concerns as legality or the opinion of parliament. Eliding 'the government' and 'the people' is a common characteristic of autocrats.[9] While the UK government was claiming its direct mandate from 'the people', the governments of Hungary and Poland were using the same rhetoric to dismantle their respective independent justice systems and persecute their political opponents.[10]

As I prepared for the Russia Report case, I knew what the government's lawyers would say in response: they represented the 'will of the people', they knew better than anyone what was in the public interest and the courts should mind their own business.

## Whitehall

The Russia Report is not the first time that executives have ignored unwritten constitutional rules. Governments have, for a long period, slowly whittled away two key 'constitutional conventions': first, the convention of ministerial responsibility and second, the convention that the civil service remains non-political.

Ministers and civil servants are accountable through the convention of individual ministerial responsibility. As Lord Morrison put it:

> When things go right ministers take the credit; when things go wrong they take the blame ... if necessary they offer their resignations.[11]

Ministers also answer to the Prime Minister. In the past the Prime Minister has acted almost cooperatively with parliament in holding ministers to account.[12]

But what happens when a Prime Minister is more interested in loyalty than integrity (or competence)? Politicians protecting their allies is not unique to the last decade. Peter Mandelson, for example, was twice forced to resign from the Blair governments. On both occasions he was rehired and promoted.[13] Since 2010, however, it has both become more common and arguably more egregious. Office seems not to be based on competence or character, but rather loyalty to the resident of Number 10.

In the decade 2010–20 David Laws, Liam Fox, Priti Patel, Amber Rudd and Gavin Williamson were all forced to resign on accusations of (variously) corruption, dishonesty, incompetence and/or endangering national security.[14] All were swiftly re-appointed or promoted.

All have one thing in common: they were close associates of the Prime Minister of the day. Their experience can be contrasted with that of other ministers who have lost their jobs in the last decade. Dominic Grieve QC was not fired as Attorney General because of incompetence or dishonesty but because he advised against withdrawing from the European Convention on Human Rights.[15] He was never rehired.

At the same time control of the civil service is increasingly centralised in 10 Downing Street.[16] After the Johnson government was returned to office in the 2019 general election, ministers were informed that their advisors would report directly to Downing Street.[17]

Johnson also centralised control over the Government Communication Service.[18] Government communications has always been problematic from a democratic perspective. The taxpayer currently funds over 4,500 public relations professionals, who promote the agenda of the government of the day.[19] Government communications professionals are not restricted simply to informing the public about what the government is doing. They also promote confidence in the government by touting its successes and spinning its failures. This amounts to a massive forced donation from taxpayers to the party in power.

The first round of centralisation occurred under the Cameron coalition, when disparate communications professionals in various departments were consolidated into a single 'Government Communication Service'.[20] Under Johnson, officers were ordered to report directly to the Prime Minister's office, thereby ensuring that civil service communications can be fully utilised by the premier's politically appointed spin doctors.

The system of holding ministers and, by extension, the entire civil service, accountable for their performance, successes and failures relies on the integrity of the Prime

Minister. If, as he did with the Russia Report, the premier chooses to ignore the unwritten rules then a vital avenue of accountability between the governors and the governed is severed. Running a government on the basis of personal loyalty to the leader is the action of an autocrat. It means that members of the government are incentivised to curry favour with their master rather than the public they exist to serve. It concentrates power in the hands of a single or small group of individuals and, as a consequence, disempowers both voters and democratic institutions.

One of our few advantages in the Russia Report case was that the security services did not bow to political pressure. In admitting that they had no objection to disclosure of the report, they gave the public the facts rather than the government's preferred bullshit. Genuine political independence in the public sector is, however, an ever rarer commodity. A range of roles in government are filled by 'public appointments'; these are individuals appointed to perform government roles who are nominally independent of ministers or the civil service. Their roles range from providing advice to oversight and even to running agencies. It is conventional that these appointments are based on expertise and experience rather than political allegiance. Indeed, an unelected executive making government appointments on the basis of political partisanship or loyalty begins to look distinctly unlike anything we would recognise as a democracy.

Public appointments are overseen by the Commissioner for Public Appointments. In November 2020 the Commissioner wrote to the chair of parliament's Committee on Standards in Public Life:

> some at the centre of government want not only to have the final say but to tilt the competition system in their favour to appoint

their allies. For instance, in recent months I have on a number of occasions had to resist, successfully so far, attempts by ministers to appoint people with clear party affiliations.[21]

The Commissioner also warned of the growth of 'unregulated appointments', by which individuals are appointed directly to public roles without any formal process. He cited the example of Baroness Harding, the Conservative peer, who was appointed, without interview, to run the NHS 'test and trace' service during the coronavirus pandemic. Harding was an interesting choice to run a service responsible for handling personal data belonging to millions of individuals. In her previous role, as CEO of TalkTalk, she was in charge during a data breach in which the confidential details of up to four million customers were leaked on the internet. The scandal cost the company £60 million and 95,000 customers and prompted the industry publication *Campaign* to declare 'Dido Harding's utter ignorance is a lesson to us all'.[22] The 'test and trace' system rarely managed to trace more than 60% of cases. By October 2020 it had almost failed completely, forcing the government to break its earlier promise to avoid a second (and, later, third) lockdown.[23]

Harding, however, was just one in a long line of political appointments to 'independent' public roles over the last decade. When Michael Gove was appointed Secretary of State for Justice, he ordered an 'independent' review of the Freedom of Information Act. Gove had made no secret of his antipathy towards the Act. As Secretary of State for Education his staff had used personal email accounts in an attempt to avoid their discussions being revealed to the public (when Hillary Clinton did the same thing as Secretary of State, it sparked some of the most expensive and long running investigations in history).

The review was, ostensibly, to be conducted by an independent panel. Gove, however, controlled the appointments to the panel. Gove's selections included Jack Straw who, as Home Secretary, had been the leading cabinet critic of the Act. He had allegedly described the committee preparing the text as 'crap fooey' and attempted to water down the legislation before it reached the floor of the Commons. Parliament had reversed many of his changes. Next up was Michael Howard who, just a few years before, had suffered public humiliation when information released under the Act revealed his extravagant use of expenses claims.[24] Finally came Patricia Hodgson, who was Deputy Chair of Ofcom when the organisation criticised the Freedom of Information Act for 'chilling' conversations between public servants.[25]

These three appointments meant that the majority of members of the review panel had publicly criticised the Freedom of Information Act before the review even began. Gove used the same tactic again when, as Chancellor of the Duchy of Lancaster, he organised the 'Independent Review of Administrative Law'.[26]

As with ministers and the civil service, public appointments are increasingly made based on loyalty to the government or even just to the Prime Minister himself. This not only breaches constitutional convention but has far more in common with the systems of patronage and personal loyalty more associated with autocracies than democracies.

## Planning

Constitutional conventions and unwritten rules are intended to keep the executive in check. They also add an important element of flexibility to parliament's powers. Parliament does not always need to use the 'sledgehammer' of an Act or even a motion, because it can use the nutcracker of convention or political pressure. When, however, the executive ceases to follow convention and, at the same time, enhances its control over parliament, government decisions become increasingly immune from accountability. This is particularly problematic because, over the course of the last decade, the executive has increasingly concentrated control among ministers and civil servants in Whitehall, excluding other accountable parts of government, like local authorities.

An archetypal example of this is planning. Planning decisions are rooted in a balance between local interests and evidence-based policymaking. Locally elected councillors (or officials who answer to them) make decisions, but must do so based on robust evidence and in accordance with the local plan set out in advance. Everyone knows where they stand, decision-makers are accountable and decisions are based on fact and reality. In my experience, the planning system is one of the best examples of effective policymaking.

When researching this book, I asked one of our most eminent constitutional lawyers, Sir Jeffrey Jowell QC, about the expansion of executive power. The first thing he said was, 'You need to look at planning.' In August 2020 the Johnson government announced its intention to 'tear down' the planning system and 'start again'.[27] Its proposed reforms will remove evidence-based decision-making and the interests of local people from their roles in the planning system and replace them with control by central government.

The Johnson government's reforms reallocate decisions about whether a development can happen from local government to central government. Local authorities will be able to determine some details of the development but not whether it happens at all. This means that decisions about whether

98

developments should take place on the Yorkshire moors, in Midlands villages or in Cornish inlets will all be taken in Whitehall.[28]

The Johnson government claims that its reforms address the national shortage of housing. When housing charity Shelter asked for the evidence and analysis behind this claim, the Secretary of State replied:

> The information you requested is not held by the Ministry of Housing, Communities and Local Government. We have undertaken work to look at various international planning systems but have not carried out any assessments falling within the scope of the request.[29]

In other words: the evidence doesn't exist.

In 2018 the Letwin Report, commissioned by the same department, concluded that the key constraint on housebuilding was not the planning system but 'the rate at which the market will absorb the homogenous product of the housebuilders' (i.e. developers don't build the houses for which they have permission). In August 2020 there were around one million homes with planning permission that had not yet been built (rather more than the 300,000 per year promised by the Johnson government).[30] The government's proposals contained no practical plan for how to actually get developers to build the houses that already have permission. It's quite clear that the Johnson planning reforms have nothing to do with solving the housing crisis and everything to do with sucking more power into the hands of the executive in Whitehall.

## Centralisation and Bullshit

I try not to get too emotionally involved in my cases. I often tell my clients that my job is to be an advocate, not an activist. It is important to maintain a degree of detachment and objectivity about the issues in the case so one can focus on doing what needs to be done to succeed in court. But the Russia Report case shocked me. The idea that a foreign government might be manipulating me at such a basic level felt like an almost inconceivable intrusion by the state into my personal decisions.

During the decade 2010–20 politicians constantly railed against state intrusion into our lives. Ministers and government-supporting think tanks all talked of 'decentralisation'. The state, we were told, should 'get out of people's way' to allow free enterprise and free will. Yet the state is now bigger, and more centralised, than at any point in the last half century. This doublespeak is just another form of political bullshit. Government made us believe it wanted to roll back the state while, in truth, doing precisely the opposite.

Local authorities are an important avenue of accountability. They ensure that, where possible, decisions are taken as close to the people they affect as possible. Parish, district and county councillors are closely rooted in (and accessible to) the communities they serve. The EU, often accused of being 'undemocratic' by critics, recognised this in establishing the legal principle of 'subsidiarity', whereby all decisions should be taken at the most local level possible.[31]

During the last decade power has been systematically transferred from local authorities to central government. From 2010 to 2020 local authority 'spending power' has fallen by 18%, primarily due to cuts in the grants that councils receive from central government.[32] Local authorities are not able to borrow money and council tax is tightly controlled, so they can only spend what central government gives them. The (ironically named) Localism Act 2011 prohibited local councils from raising council tax by more than 2% per year unless a referendum was held (no such fetters apply to the national government's own powers of taxation).[33] In 2013 the Treasury claimed it would empower local authorities by allowing them to keep 50% of the business rates they collected. In fact, the government forced local authorities to pay back far more than 50% whenever it decided that the authority did not need the money. The cuts to local authority grants hit metropolitan areas (which are statistically least likely to vote for the Conservative Party) the hardest.[34]

Universal Credit, introduced as part of the Cameron coalition's promise to 'roll back the state', transferred power over housing benefit from local authorities to the Department for Work and Pensions.[35] In the name of 'democratising education' the Cameron coalition introduced 'free schools' in 2010 and expanded previous (Labour) governments' academies programmes. While ordinary schools answer to local government, free schools and academies are controlled directly by the Department for Education.[36] Central government was also given powers to force state schools to become free schools or academies.[37] In 2014 control was further centralised under the command of eight 'regional schools commissioners', who report directly to the Secretary of State. The majority of free schools are now consolidated in large 'chains', in which decisions are taken by unaccountable trustees.

The coronavirus pandemic provided a golden opportunity for the executive to expand its power at the expense of parliament. As Levitsky and Ziblatt note:

Crises are hard to predict, but their political consequences are not. They facilitate the concentration and, very often, abuse of power. Wars and terrorist attacks produce a 'rally 'round the flag' effect in which public support for the government increases – often dramatically.[38]

National emergencies pose difficult constitutional questions. On the one hand it makes sense to give the executive extraordinary powers so that it can deal with the crisis as quickly and effectively as possible. On the other, concentrating power in the hands of the executive is a recipe for abuse. As the *New York Times* observed:

> Governments and rights groups agree that these extraordinary times call for extraordinary measures . . .
>
> But critics say some governments are using the public health crisis as cover to seize new powers that have little to do with the outbreak, with few safeguards to ensure that their new authority will not be abused.[39]

Parliament was willing to confer unprecedented peacetime powers on the executive. The Coronavirus Act 2020 allowed the government, without consulting parliament, to cancel elections, restrict or ban public gatherings and increase surveillance of citizens not suspected of criminal offences. It also allowed the executive to detain anyone who 'may be' infected with the virus. Given that literally anyone in the world 'may be' infected, this is, in practice, a power to arbitrarily detain anyone without trial. Ian Dunt, editor of Politics.co.uk, described the Act as 'the most extensive encroachment on British civil liberties we have ever seen outside of wartime'.[40]

When the Act was passed, Boris Johnson claimed that the

UK would 'turn the tide' of the pandemic in just twelve weeks. The Coronavirus Act, however, granted his government extraordinary powers for at least two years (this was eventually cut to six months), renewable by a simple up or down vote in parliament. In October 2020 parliament renewed the powers. The story, however, has a twist: none of the powers in the Coronavirus Act were actually necessary. Many of its provisions broadly replicate those in the Civil Contingencies Act 2004. The 2004 Act, however, contains a special hybrid scrutiny procedure, which allows the government to make decisions quickly but keeps parliament in the loop. The Coronavirus Act just did away with the parliamentary scrutiny. Its effect, then, was not to give the executive the powers necessary to fight the pandemic, but rather to remove avenues of accountability for the government's existing emergency powers.

Despite its new suite of unaccountable powers, the government did not take any significant action to respond to the pandemic until the end of March 2020. When it did, it used an entirely different piece of legislation, the Public Health Act 1984, to impose a national lockdown. As the pandemic progressed the government introduced various new sets of regulations using the Public Health Act. Parliament was given little choice about whether to approve these new laws. Many of the regulations were announced just minutes before they came into effect. Tom Hickman QC described the various lockdown regulations as 'the most severe restrictions on liberty ever imposed'.[41] Parliament was reduced to the role of bystander.[42]

## The End of the Russia Report Case

The courts, for the most part, still deal in reality rather than rhetoric so I thought it unlikely that they would buy a defence based solely on the government's claims to an imaginary 'direct mandate'. There was, however, a better argument that the government could make: that age-old chestnut – national security. No matter how good the rest of our case was, the government could press the 'national security button' and we wouldn't stand a chance. This is another unwritten rule of the constitution. The courts will generally take the government at its word on questions of national security on the understanding that the government will not say something is 'a matter of national security' unless it really is. But what happens when the government abuses this privilege?

In the Russia Report case, we found out. We knew the government would claim that releasing the report would risk national security (even though the leaks from the security services suggested otherwise). We had to find a witness who could explain that releasing the report would not pose a risk. Intelligence sources, while willing to give quotes to journalists, were not prepared to give evidence in court. Neither were the members of the ISC. With time running out and the election approaching, we had to accept that this was not a case we could win.

The report was finally released more than six months later (after the Johnson government failed in its attempt to force the ISC to accept its candidate, Chris Grayling, for chair). It revealed that the government had shredded constitutional convention by politicising intelligence gathering. There is a certain irony in the fact that we backed out of our legal claim because we knew the court would defer to the government on questions of national security. The report exposed the executive's extraordinary negligence in that very area.

The document showed the government knew about the risk of Russian interference in 2016. Yet the executive refused to investigate interference in elections won by the government or its supporters. Although the report is heavily redacted, it appears to show that the security services gathered information about the 2014 referendum on Scottish independence but not the 2016 Brexit referendum.[43] The leaders of the winning 'Vote Leave' campaign joined the government en masse after 2016. The report stated:

> We have not been provided with any post-referendum assessment of Russian attempts at interference . . . This situation is in stark contrast to the US handling of allegations of Russian interference in the 2016 presidential election, where an intelligence community assessment was produced within two months of the vote, with an unclassified summary being made public . . .
>
> Had the relevant parts of the intelligence community conducted a similar threat assessment prior to the referendum, it is inconceivable that they would not have reached the same conclusion as to Russian intent, which might then have led them to take action to protect the process.[44]

The committee noted that publicly available studies pointed to Russian interference in the 2016 referendum, including 'the preponderance of pro-Brexit or anti-EU stories' in Russian sponsored English-language media, as well as 'bots' and 'trolls' on social media. The report concluded that ministers had, in effect, turned a blind eye to Russian activities.[45]

In response to the report, the Johnson government claimed that it 'had seen no evidence of successful interference in the EU referendum'. As Stuart Hosie, a member of the ISC, pointed out:

The UK Government have actively avoided looking for evidence that Russia interfered. We were told that they hadn't seen any evidence, but that is meaningless if they hadn't looked for it.[46]

As the Russia Report case showed, there is no legal remedy for these failures. The government can ignore conventions with impunity unless parliament steps in and forces it to stop. Thus far MPs have been unwilling or unable to do so. The result is that longstanding constitutional rules, which should ensure that ministers and civil servants take responsibility for their actions, have become increasingly meaningless. At the same time, after a decade of centralisation, the executive now exercises more power than at any point in the last half century.

# 6

# KEEPING SECRETS

*Information . . . assists in combatting poverty, oppression, corruption, prejudice and inefficiency.*
        Lord Mance, Kennedy v Information
        Commissioner [2015] AC 455, cited
        in Stanley v Information Commissioner
        and Secretary of State for Northern Ireland

On 21 November 1974 two bombs exploded in Birmingham city centre.[1] The first (at 20.17) in the Mulberry Bush, a pub on the ground floor of an office block next to New Street Station. The second (at 20.27) in the Tavern on the Town, a basement bar in one of Birmingham's busiest shopping destinations. A third bomb was later found near Hagley Road, having failed to detonate. Twenty-one people were killed and a further 182 injured.[2] My father, then a student at Birmingham University, heard the explosions from campus, nearly two miles away. This chapter is about how the government, nearly fifty years later, continues to fight to keep the truth about the Birmingham Pub Bombings (and many other things) secret. It concerns our first theme: accountability – and how the government evades it.

The Provisional IRA (PIRA) claimed responsibility for the

Birmingham bombings. Later six men were convicted of the crime.[3] Over the next two decades it emerged that the Birmingham Six had been falsely imprisoned. Their 'confessions' were obtained by torture, the forensic evidence was flawed and their convictions were fundamentally unsafe. In 1991 their convictions were overturned and they were set free. Michael Mansfield QC wrote a compelling description of the case in his book *Memoirs of a Radical Lawyer*.[4] I read Mansfield's account while I was teaching at the University of Birmingham to fund my PhD studies. It was one of the things that inspired me to practise human rights law.

The Birmingham Six were not responsible for the bombings. But someone was. The real bombers have never been caught. After the Six were released the authorities seemed to lose interest in the case. Left without answers about who killed their loved ones, and without the closure of a proper conviction, the families of the victims began to demand justice. They formed a campaign group, Justice 4 the 21, to persuade the government to deliver an effective investigation. In 2019 the government agreed to hold an inquest into the bombings. The coroner, however, refused to consider the question of who was responsible.[5]

J421's solicitor, Christopher Stanley, began investigating himself. He requested a file from the Northern Ireland Office entitled 'CJ4/6052: Provisional IRA intentions and activities in Great Britain'. The file related to 1975, the year after the bombings. Christopher knew it probably wouldn't contain 'a smoking gun'. He suspected, however, that it would have information about the 'political thinking and the reaction to the mainland terror campaign post the pub bombings' and give insight into 'what was happening in the context of the time'. The Northern Ireland Office (NIO) refused to let Christopher see the file, citing reasons of 'national security'.[6] When the Information Commissioner supported the government's refusal to release the information, Christopher's only option was to challenge the decision in court. He asked me to represent him and, together, we started to build our case. We knew that it would ultimately come down to one very simple question: how important is transparency?

## Transparency as a Constitutional Value

Transparency has not been recognised as a 'constitutional principle' in the same way as parliamentary sovereignty or the rule of law. Like these concepts, however, it is an essential element of a liberal society. If a state has a monopoly on information, no one can question its decisions. As Alexis de Tocqueville put it:

> the concentration of power and the subjection of individuals will increase amongst democratic nations ... in the same proportion as their ignorance.[7]

James Madison, charged with writing the US constitution, expanded Tocqueville's point:

> A popular Government without popular information or the means of acquiring it, is but a Prologue to a Farce or a Tragedy or perhaps both. Knowledge will forever govern ignorance, and a people who mean to be their own governors must arm themselves with the power which knowledge gives.[8]

The UK historically had a rather cold relationship with transparency. Until 2005 the publication of government information was governed solely by the Official Secrets Acts. These effectively established a presumption against transparency and imposed draconian punishments on anyone who disclosed information without permission. Behind this statutory wall of silence were concealed a multitude of sins. Ian Cobain, in his history of the British state's battles over transparency, *The History Thieves*, describes various attempts by officials to keep voters in the dark about the reality of government activities. They include the destruction of hundreds of thousands of colonial records during the retreat from the former British empire, a war in Sudan fought almost entirely in secret and a warehouse complex in Hanslope containing miles of military files kept in legal limbo to avoid scrutiny.[9]

As the UK transitioned to a more genuinely democratic nation during the twentieth century, citizens began to demand better access to information. If we don't know what our government is doing and why, then we can't ensure it answers for its actions. This has long been recognised by other democratic states. The United States passed freedom of information legislation in 1966. President Lyndon B. Johnson,* on adding his signature, stated:

> This legislation springs from one of our most essential principles: a democracy works best when the people have all the information that the security of the nation will permit.[10]

---

* Some recent scholarship suggests that Johnson was personally sceptical about transparency and opposed the legislation when he was in Congress. Nevertheless (whether or not reluctantly), he signed the substantive legislation as president. See https://lawresearchguides.cwru.edu/c.php?g=669890 and Belmas, G., and Overbeck, W., *Major Principles of Media Law* (New York: Cengage, 2014), p. 394.

New Zealand, Australia and Canada all adopted freedom of information laws between 1982 and 1983. In Sweden, such laws have been in place since 1766. UK governments nevertheless resisted calls for equivalent legislation throughout the 1980s and early 1990s. As Tony Blair put it, a 'culture of secrecy permeate[d] almost every single aspect of government activity'.[11]

The tide turned with the election of the Blair government in 1997. Blair, in the early years of his premiership, appeared to genuinely believe in constitutional reform, including freedom of information. In March 1996 he told transparency campaigners:

> Information is power and any government's attitude about sharing information with the people actually says a great deal about how it views power itself, and how it views the relationship between itself and the people who elected it. Does the government regard people's involvement in politics as being restricted to periodic elections? Or does it regard itself as in some sense in a genuine partnership with people? The government's attitude to what it is prepared to tell people and the knowledge it will share with them says a great deal about where it stands on that matter.[12]

In 1999 the Blair government published its white paper on freedom of information. It proposed a law requiring officials to disclose information on request unless doing so caused harm to one of seven defined interests.[13] The Bill that made its way to the floor of the house in December 1999 fell somewhat short of the promise in the white paper. In the intervening period the Blair government had been wracked by its first scandal. In November 1997 the *Sunday Telegraph* revealed that Formula One boss Bernie Ecclestone, a major donor, had lobbied for an exemption from the government's ban on tobacco advertising. Ecclestone got his exemption and people started to ask whether major donors were able to buy influence with the government.[14] The Bill introduced to the floor of the house contained more exemptions than the white paper and new clauses that appeared to run directly against the spirit of the legislation. One, in particular, would have banned the recipient of information from sharing it with others.

As the Bill completed its parliamentary stages, many of the more egregious clauses were removed. The text that reached the statute book was not perfect, but it nevertheless represented a complete volte-face from the previous default to secrecy. The Act removed the presumption against disclosure. Lord Sumption, giving judgment in the Supreme Court in *Kennedy v Information Commissioner* (a case to which we will return momentarily), summed up the significance of the Act:

> The Freedom of Information Act 2000 was a landmark enactment of great constitutional significance for the United Kingdom. It introduced a new regime governing the disclosure of information held by public authorities. It created a prima facie right to the disclosure of all such information, save in so far as that right was qualified by the terms of the Act or the information in question was exempt. The qualifications and exemptions embody a careful balance between the public interest considerations militating for and against disclosure.[15]

The Freedom of Information Act is not the only right to information. Transparency has been a key tenet of the justice system since the days of (attempted) absolute monarchy. As Lord Justice Toulson (later Lord Toulson) put it in *R (Guardian News Media Ltd) v Westminster Magistrates Court*:

Open justice. The words express a principle at the heart of our system of justice and vital to the rule of law. The rule of law is a fine concept, but fine words butter no parsnips. How is the rule of law itself to be policed? It is an age-old question. *Quis custodiet ipsos custodes*: who will guard the guards themselves? In a democracy, where power depends on the consent of the people governed, the answer must lie in the transparency of the legal process. Open justice lets in the light and allows the public to scrutinise the workings of the law, for better or for worse . . .

This is a constitutional principle which has been recognised by the common law since the fall of the Stuart dynasty, as Lord Shaw explained. It is not only the individual judge who is open to scrutiny but the process of justice.[16]

Unfortunately, the Freedom of Information Act could not cure the government of its allergy to daylight. The executive has been trying to wriggle out of the Act almost from the moment it received royal assent. Blair immediately regretted his support. Transparency, it transpired, caused too many political headaches:

[In Opposition] we made a very big mistake in allowing the impression to be gained that we were going to be better than the Tories; not just better at governing, but more moral, more upright . . . What I failed to realise is that we would also have our skeletons rattling around the cupboard, and while they might be different, they would be just as repulsive. Moreover, I did not at that time see the full implications of the massive increase in transparency we were planning as part of our reforms to 'clean up politics'. For the first time, details of donors and the amounts given to political parties were going to be published. I completely missed the fact that though in Opposition millionaire donors were to be welcomed as a sign of respectability, in government they would very quickly be seen as buying influence.[17]

The Act, which came into force in 2005, was initially relatively effective. After the turn of the decade, however, compliance nosedived. In 2010 just under 40% of requests were wholly or partially refused. By 2018 it was nearly 60%.[18] The Department for Exiting the European Union, the Department for International Trade and the Department for Business, Energy and Industrial Strategy each granted fewer than 30% of requests in full.[19]

Some departments and ministers embraced various convoluted schemes to avoid having to disclose information. As mentioned earlier, when Michael Gove was Secretary of State for Education, his staff used personal email accounts to avoid having their emails subject to FOI (free legal advice: this doesn't actually work).[20] In August 2020 Reuters reported that the Secretary of State for International Trade, Liz Truss, had deleted references to the Institute for Economic Affairs, which campaigns on trade issues, from the public record of her meetings.[21] Around the same time that the deleted meetings occurred, a Charity Commission investigation found the IEA had broken the law by campaigning for a 'hard Brexit' while claiming to be an education charity.[22] Truss claimed that the meetings were 'personal'. Civil servants in various departments have, when confronted in the Information Tribunal, suggested they will stop keeping records if they are forced to disclose information. This would constitute a breach of the Civil Service Code.

## Excuses, Excuses, Excuses

For the most part, however, behind the scenes machinations are unnecessary because the Freedom of Information Act itself is relatively ineffective in the face of an executive determined to avoid transparency. It contains so many exemptions, and these have been interpreted so broadly by the courts, that government is often able to lawfully avoid disclosing information. The government has fed requesters, the Information Commissioner and the Tribunal an increasingly absurd series of reasons as to why information falls within exemptions. Those who claim that the courts 'interfere in politics' need only spend a few days in the Tribunal to see how wrong they are. In the interests of 'not interfering in politics', tribunals are often willing to accept even the most outlandish explanations from government officials. Coincidentally, the exemptions only seem to apply when the information might be embarrassing to the government.

The Birmingham case (now named *Stanley v Information Commissioner*) was no exception. The Northern Ireland Office claimed that disclosing the information would somehow put the UK's security at risk from 'terrorism'. It was suggested that disclosure might provoke revenge attacks against informers named in the documents. Christopher suggested that the names be redacted. Nevertheless, the government maintained its position.

The PIRA, the subject of the file, declared a ceasefire in 1992. By 2005 the Independent International Commission on Decommissioning had reported that the PIRA had decommissioned the totality of its weapons.[23] The PIRA has not launched an attack in more than two decades. Its erstwhile leadership cooperated with Chris Mullin's investigation of the bombings and even gave evidence at the 2018 inquest.[24] The organisation is believed to have given Mullin the names of all of the bombers on the condition that he did not disclose them until after their deaths. The supposed 'threat' to national security relied on by the government was, therefore, comprised of a defunct organisation without any weapons, the remnants of which had already cooperated with the investigation.

*Stanley* is not, however, the strangest example of government agencies relying on historical 'threats' to avoid disclosing information. In 1998 the Tribunal considered the case of a historian who had requested information from Special Branch concerning its monitoring of anarchist groups in mainland Europe between 1888 and 1912. The Metropolitan Police claimed that disclosure would put law enforcement at risk because disclosing the names of nineteenth-century anarchist informers would make modern-day informers less likely to come forward.

On this occasion the Commissioner and Tribunal didn't buy the story and the Met was compelled to publish the files (albeit with the names of the informers redacted). In 2011 a former police officer named John Marriott asked the Met to disclose files from the same era relating to the Whitechapel murders. Once again, the Met claimed that disclosing the names of people who assisted the investigation would put off possible modern-day informants.[25] The Commissioner and Tribunal both upheld the Met's refusal.[26] Put bluntly: both the statutory regulator and a court of law accepted the excuse that the publication of the Met's Jack the Ripper files would jeopardise investigations more than a century later.

A favourite government argument is that ministers and civil servants need a 'safe space' to have 'frank' discussions about policy. The government is, of course, virulently against 'safe spaces' when its political opponents may benefit. When London

Young Labour established a small room as a 'safe space' at its 2018 annual general meeting (intended for people with disabilities to take a break from the crowd), the Conservative Party Vice Chair, Ben Bradley, mocked the group on Twitter.[27] And when, in 2016, a number of universities established 'safe spaces' for debate (in which contributors would not be permitted to make racist or homophobic remarks) Theresa May (then Prime Minister) told the House of Commons:

> I think everybody is finding this concept of safe spaces quite extraordinary, frankly.[28]

There are small differences between the 'safe spaces' that the government likes and those it doesn't. Safe spaces for ministers and civil servants allegedly allow them to speak freely because they don't have to worry about their remarks being made public. And safe spaces at universities allow students from minorities to speak freely because they don't need to worry about being abused. The difference, of course, is that the latter protect private individuals belonging to marginalised groups from oppression, while the former protect public officials who are supposed to be accountable to the public.

Ultimately the safe space argument in FOI cases is about the government wanting to treat the electorate like children. It relies on the assumption that the voting public can't be trusted to respect ministers and officials having frank conversations about public policy. This distrust of the public was clear in one of my first freedom of information cases. I represented a journalist investigating the failure of an academy trust. The trust suffered financial difficulties for a number of years and consistently received poor reports from Ofsted. Eventually it collapsed completely. My client discovered that the Chief Executive of the trust had repeatedly lied about his experience. He claimed to have held a number of senior positions at global companies, many of which turned out to be entirely fictitious.[29] My client wanted to know what background checks the Department for Education had undertaken, why it believed that the trust and its CEO were competent to run academies and what measures it had taken once Ofsted reported its concerns and the trust ran into financial difficulties.[30]

The Department for Education claimed that it could not release the information because officials needed a 'safe space' to discuss failing academy chains. If forced to disclose such information, it argued, then officials could not give frank and objective advice to ministers. A senior DfE official gave evidence at the hearing. In cross-examination, I challenged her on the necessity of a 'safe space':

SF: You're aware of the Civil Service Code?

Witness: Yes.

SF: You're aware that it forms part of your contract of employment?

W: Yes.

SF: So, you're aware that if you breach the Code, you breach your contract of employment?

W: Yes.

SF: The Code is included in the Authorities Bundle at Tab A4. You will see that you are required to be honest, objective and not to hold back inconvenient information.

W: Yes.

SF: You will see that obligation is not contingent on what you say being kept secret.

W: Yes.

SF: Do you comply with the Code?

W: Yes.

SF: You give advice that is honest and objective?

W: Yes.

SF: You don't hold back inconvenient facts or opinions?

W: No, I do not.

SF: When necessary you speak freely and frankly?

W: Yes.

SF: Would you say you comply with the Code more than your colleagues?

W: No. I think my colleagues comply with the Code.

SF: Did you comply with the Code in relation to the information in question?

W: Yes.

SF: Did your colleagues?

W: Yes.

SF: If the information in question here is made public will you breach your contractual obligations in the future?

W: No.

SF: So you don't need a 'safe space' to talk freely and frankly, do you? Because giving frank advice is your job.[31]

How is the government able to get away with making such ridiculous arguments? There are two principal reasons. First, the courts have adopted a presumption that the government is competent and, consequently, give its witness evidence special weight. The rationale for this rule was explained in a case called *All-Party Parliamentary Group on Extraordinary Rendition v Information Commissioner*. In that case the Tribunal was asked to decide whether disclosure of certain information would prejudice international relations. The Tribunal explained:

In practical terms, the Foreign Secretary has unrestricted access to full and open advice from his experienced advisors, both in the Foreign Office and the intelligence services. He is accordingly far better informed, as well as having far more relevant experience, than any judge, for the purpose of assessing the likely attitude and action of foreign intelligence services as a result of publication of the redacted paragraphs, and the consequences of such actions so far as the prevention of terrorism in this country is concerned.[33]

This is all very well when one is dealing with the sort of assessment that requires the help of experienced intelligence officials. But the reasoning makes sense only so far as the executive really is competent. As has been repeatedly shown, it often isn't. Indeed, in many cases freedom of information requests are made with the purpose of exposing government incompetence. The court's approach makes it incredibly difficult for citizens to ensure the government respects our rights. No matter how absurd the explanation, or how obviously incompetent the minister or civil servant, the courts generally afford them greater deference than they do internationally renowned experts called by citizens. This makes accountability more a matter of theory than practice.

In *Stanley* we called Professor Mark McGovern to give evidence about the risk to national security if the files were released. McGovern is a professor of sociology at Edge Hill University and a member of Queen Mary University of London's state crime initiative. He has spent more than fifteen years studying violent terrorists in Northern Ireland and has published numerous books, articles and lectures on the subject. He gave evidence that the threat posed by the PIRA was next to nonexistent. Against McGovern, the government called an official from the NIO. He was a good witness. He didn't overstate his case and seemed, at least, to have thought carefully about his assessment. In my experience, government witnesses, when compelled to answer questions from the other side, tend to adopt an attitude of passive-aggressive evasiveness. I am often left feeling that they are wearily tolerating my impudence in questioning them. In this instance, however, our cross-examination proceeded more like a friendly chat. There was, however, one crucial point that I saved until the end:

SF: You say that disclosing this information will increase the risk of a terrorist attack or attacks against informers.

W: Yes.

SF: The NIO has made this claim before, hasn't it?

W: I don't understand.

SF: This is not the first case in which the NIO has said disclosing information would increase the risk of terrorist attacks or attacks on informants, is it?

W: No.

SF: In fact, you often rely on this argument.

W: Yes, so far as I know.

SF: It doesn't always work though, does it?

W: What do you mean?

SF: In some of the cases in which you have relied on this argument, you have been successful but in others you have not.

W: [No response]

SF: That's correct, isn't it?

W: Yes.

SF: So, there are some cases in which you have said information will, if released, increase the risk of attacks and that information has been released anyway.

W: Yes.

SF: Can you give an example of when information has been

released, contrary to your submissions, and it has led to a
terrorist attack?

W: [After a pause] No.

SF: Can you give an example of when it has led to an attack on
an informer?

W: [Another pause] Not right now.

SF: Can you give an example of when any information concerning legacy issues, released under the Freedom of Information
Act, has led to any negative consequence for national
security?

W: [Another pause] No. I cannot.[33]

I have asked some version of these questions in almost every
freedom of information case in which I have acted. Whenever a
government witness has alleged that prejudice to a particular
national interest would flow from disclosure of information, I
have asked them to give an example of where that sort of prejudice has occurred in practice. Not once has a witness been able
to do so.

The second reason that tribunals so often buy the government's stories is that the person requesting disclosure is not
allowed to see all of the evidence. Because of the nature of the
freedom of information process, the requester can't see the
withheld information until the Tribunal orders the government
to release it. The government, however, is also allowed to give
much of its evidence in secret. This makes it impossible to test or
question much of the government's evidence. In theory the
Information Commissioner and the Tribunal can ask questions
on the requester's behalf during the 'closed' session. This is no
substitute for having the requester's own barrister conduct questioning. The Information Commissioner often supports the
government, so relying on the Commissioner's representative

means the requester must rely on their opponent to make their case for them. This is rarely effective. The Tribunal itself rarely subjects witnesses to forensic questioning. Indeed, in one case, a judge asked me to stop my cross-examination because I was being too 'forensic'.

## Culture of Concealment

In one of the cases described in this chapter, it was subsequently revealed that the government spent at least £50,000 resisting disclosing the information.[34] Why is the government so desperate to keep information secret? In one department, at least, it just seems to be part of the culture. As one former civil servant told the Tribunal (in a different case in which I was involved):

> During my work on [an international trade agreement] I was involved in responding to Freedom of Information requests. While working for government my impression was the start point for responding was 'how little can we get away with releasing'.

The government insists that it needs to maintain its veil of secrecy in order to govern effectively but, in practice, it often does more harm than good. In *Stanley* Professor McGovern explained:

> Truth-recovery is considered a central mechanism in the Truth and Reconciliation process. It serves the needs of the relatives of victims and survivors in providing answers to their questions thus enabling a semblance of understanding. It serves the post-Conflict society in fulfilling the expectations which were created when the peace came . . .
>
> National Security should not be used as an excuse to obscure

access to the truth regarding the legacy of the conflict if what it protects could contribute to the out-workings of the truth which is essential to the peace process.[35]

He went on to explain that the government's aversion to transparency poses a greater threat to national security than the disclosure of the file in question. The process of truth and reconciliation is essential to enabling communities in Northern Ireland to come to terms with the Troubles. The government's refusal to disclose information about historic atrocities stymies this process and consequently increases the risk of friction between communities.

The government's culture of secrecy was to have tragic consequences during the coronavirus pandemic. In the early 1990s, when facing a public health crisis caused by BSE ('mad cow disease'), the government pursued a strategy of only revealing the bare minimum of information. This was criticised by the public inquiry into the crisis. In the wake of the review, with the BSE crisis still ongoing, Professor Chris Higgins was appointed to chair a new advisory group called the Spongiform Encephalopathy Advisory Committee (SEAC). This performed a similar role to that played by the Scientific Advisory Group for Emergencies (SAGE), during the coronavirus pandemic. SEAC held all of its meetings in public, published its data and limited its membership to scientists (although ministers and officials were welcome to attend and ask questions).[36]

From the start of the coronavirus pandemic, SAGE discarded the lessons learned from BSE. It met in secret, its members were banned from disclosing the content of its discussions and, for several months, the government refused even to reveal its membership. Professor Sir Paul Nurse is highly critical of the 'shroud of secrecy' drawn around major decisions, particularly those taken early in the pandemic. He describes decision-making as happening in a 'black box' comprising a few chosen scientists, officials and ministers.[37] Given that Nurse is the former president of the Royal Society, chief scientific advisor to the European Commission, director of the Francis Crick Institute and a Nobel laureate, his views should carry some weight.

The government concealed important information from the public and gave misleading statements on important issues. In January 2020 a government spokesperson assured the public that the country was 'well prepared for any new diseases'. This turned out to be a lie.[38] The most recent test of the government's pandemic preparedness (in 2016, codenamed Cygnus) identified a substantial number of shortfalls, including a lack of personal protective equipment (PPE). Sure enough, when the pandemic hit, the NHS was so short of PPE that doctors and nurses had to make do with bin bags in place of masks or overalls.[39] Cygnus's long list of recommendations was never implemented.[40] Early in the pandemic the government claimed to be doing all the testing necessary. This was another lie. Testing capacity was so low that the first 'test and trace' efforts collapsed within weeks. As Nurse put it:

> They seemed not to want to admit that they weren't prepared, that they were unable to do the testing properly, because that would have been an admission of failure from square one.[41]

Nurse argues that the government's secrecy-first approach actually caused mistakes. Accountable government facilitates better decision-making. When decisions and analysis are not subjected to scrutiny, the decision-makers are much more likely to make errors. One example was the decision to attempt to build giant 'lighthouse' testing labs from scratch, rather than make use of existing capacity. As Nurse told the *Guardian*, anyone with an understanding of the testing process could have told officials that the plan was unworkable well before time and money were wasted. The decision was, however, made in secret, meaning that the government plugged away for months trying to get an unworkable system off the ground.[42]

The government's attitude to transparency was also laced with tragic irony. In February and March officials opposed a national lockdown because they thought the public was unlikely to comply. Reading the SAGE minutes from that period, it does not appear to have occurred to anyone to simply explain the severity of the pandemic to the public. Ultimately, once news overtook the government's communications, the public itself demanded a lockdown.[43] The executive's instinct, to treat the electorate like children, was proved decisively wrong. Neil Ferguson, Professor of Mathematical Biology at Imperial College, has suggested that had the government instituted a lockdown just a week earlier the Covid-19 death toll could have been reduced by as much as half.[44] The government's distrust of the public may have cost tens of thousands of lives.

We lost the Birmingham case. Among other things, the Tribunal agreed with the government on the question of national security, finding 'it is clear there continues to be a national security threat from dissident republicans'. It did not engage with Professor McGovern's argument that this had nothing to do with the PIRA or the government witnesses' own admission that there had never been a threat to national security as a result of the disclosure of information of that type. While the Tribunal 'considered with the greatest care the public interest points', it decided that the truth and reconciliation process was 'unlikely to benefit from material about IRA activity and intentions in

Great Britain'. There was no mention of the fact that victims of the Troubles had lived in Great Britain as well as Northern Ireland (and, indeed, one even gave evidence to the Tribunal during that case!).

Three months after the case ended the government imposed a moratorium on most investigations of legacy crimes in Northern Ireland.[45] We will, in all likelihood, never find out the extent of the crimes committed by the British state or various terrorist groups. The government's decision largely ended any hope victims had of uncovering the truth.

The role of transparency in a democratic constitution boils down to one very simple question: Are citizens allowed to know the truth about what their government is doing? A government which rejects transparency is a government which does not trust its citizens. A government which does not trust its citizens is always frightening.

# 7

# BRITS ABROAD

> . . . *the powers available to Parliament to scrutinise*
> *ministers' actions [in international relations] are*
> *anachronistic and inadequate.*
> House of Lords Constitution Committee, HL345

Waiting to speak to a parliamentary committee feels a bit like waiting to be called into the headteacher's office. You sit on a bench in a long wood-panelled corridor with a stone floor and a threadbare carpet (admittedly a nicer corridor than the one in my old school). I was sandwiched between Professors Lorand Bartels (Cambridge) and James Harrison (Warwick). We were there to give evidence to parliament's Joint Committee on Human Rights. Bartels and Harrison were both seasoned veterans of the select committee hearing, but it was my first time. I resisted the urge to take a selfie.

The committee was investigating whether the UK constitution properly protected fundamental rights in respect of international trade agreements. It concluded that the UK's mechanisms for scrutinising treaties were 'inadequate'.[1] A few weeks later the House of Lords Constitution Committee concluded that the same provisions were 'limited and flawed'.[2] This was in

2019. Just three years earlier the government had promised to restore the UK's 'sovereignty' and allow parliament and the people to 'take back control'. A year later, on the day the UK officially left the EU, Boris Johnson celebrated the UK's 'recaptured sovereignty'.[3] We were led to believe that 'recapturing' our 'sovereignty' was a form of empowerment. In reality, it was precisely the opposite. The fiction of 'sovereignty' has long been used to exclude citizens from government and allow the executive to conduct foreign policy almost entirely without oversight.

Two weeks after the UK left the EU, I was involved with a case that exposed just how far the government will go to avoid scrutiny.* In 2016 the journalist Brendan Montague, working with an NGO called Global Justice Now, began investigating secret trade talks called 'trade working groups'. Trade agreements can determine whether and on what terms we can do business in other countries. But they can also dictate our environmental standards, health and safety measures, healthcare provision, food standards, and impact on almost every area of public policy.

The government refused to tell him who it was negotiating with, what was on the agenda, who attended or what was discussed, so Brendan challenged them under the Freedom of Information Act. During the week-long hearing, a series of experts (with whom the Tribunal ultimately substantially agreed) explained how the government can conduct international relations without democratic scrutiny. This comes down

---

* During the time that I was on sabbatical writing this book, this case went to appeal. At the time of writing, I am not acting in the appeal and have not seen any of the papers. This chapter deals only with the (publicly available) matters raised and decision at first instance.

to one of our four themes: enfranchisement. If citizens are excluded from foreign policy decisions, then we lose control over a significant area of our government which directly affects our lives.

## Sovereignty vs Democracy

The concept of 'sovereignty', as it's still used today, originated as a way for autocratic monarchs to keep control of their realms. It dates back to the Peace of Westphalia in 1648, which ended the Thirty Years War.[4] The war had been fought largely over which religion should dominate Europe. In the Westphalia treaties it was agreed that the monarch would have the right to determine the religion of the state. Over the following centuries this evolved to mean that states are entitled to complete control of their internal affairs and are basically equal contracting parties in international relations. As Hedley Bull famously put it, a sovereign state has no internal equal and no external superior.[5] In practice this means that whoever controls the government of the state can exercise the state's sovereignty. International organisations, like the UN or EU, have no right to 'interfere' in the internal affairs of sovereign states.

An alternative form of sovereignty is 'popular' or 'democratic' sovereignty. In this version, sovereignty belongs to 'the nation' or 'the people'. As James Madison put it:

> governments are in fact but different agents and trustees of the people.[6]

In this version, there is no need for states to be the only actors in international relations. It has space for international laws and institutions that empower individuals rather than states.[7] After the Second World War the international community recognised that the pure Westphalian version of sovereignty gave governments too much power over the people. Global human rights treaties and international organisations like the UN, the WTO and the EU represent an acknowledgement that popular sovereignty (which prioritises the rights of citizens) is a better guarantee of international peace and domestic democracy than Westphalian sovereignty.[8]

The UK, however, is governed on a model far closer to autocratic Westphalian sovereignty than the democratic sovereignty envisaged by Madison. Foreign policy falls within the royal prerogative, exercised on the monarch's behalf by the Prime Minister and other members of the government. This allows the executive to effectively do what it likes in the realm of international relations without answering to parliament or citizens. Under the Blair and Brown governments some moves were made to democratise foreign policy. Blair and Brown voluntarily sought parliament's consent to major foreign policy decisions like the interventions in Afghanistan and Iraq. Since 2016 that approach has been abandoned. The May and Johnson governments both went to court to prevent parliament from 'interfering' in foreign policy, first in *Miller I* (where the Supreme Court held that, as leaving the EU meant changing domestic law, parliament had to have a vote) and again in *Vince* (the Benn Act case discussed in Chapter 3).

In *Montague*, we needed to convince the court that transparency was in the public interest. Brendan and I, along with his excellent solicitor (Erin Alcock of Leigh Day), agreed that our best chance of winning his case was to show the Tribunal just how undemocratic the UK's approach to foreign policy was. We asked Newcastle University's Dr Sylvia de Mars, an expert in constitutional and international trade law, to lay out the situation. Sylvia explained that the executive can bind the UK to a treaty in international law without a vote in parliament. While, formally, it must first lay the treaty before parliament for twenty days, the executive can use its control of the parliamentary time-table to ensure that MPs never vote.[9] Even if they do get a chance to vote, legislators can only delay, not reject, ratification of the treaty. In theory, parliament's consent is required to implement the agreement in domestic law. Once it has ratified a treaty, however, the government has signed the UK up to a full range of repercussions if the treaty is breached (including fines and even international sanctions). Parliament can thus effectively be strong-armed into passing the government's chosen measures. As the Tribunal concluded:

> we are quite convinced that Dr de Mars is right when she says that, regardless of the strict legal position, in practice once a free trade agreement has been finalised with a foreign state Parliament and the government are likely to follow it and the law of the UK is likely to be amended accordingly.[10]

This is far less democratic than (for example) the EU's approach (from which the UK also benefitted before Brexit). The European Parliament is empowered to approve or reject any treaty signed by the Union. It can also approve or reject the negotiating mandate before talks begin and is entitled to regular updates about progress.* When the UK was a member of the

---

* It's worth noting that MPs had the opportunity to change this by voting for an amendment to the Trade Bill 2019–21 that would have given them a say in international treaties. Legislators voted down the amendment, thereby choosing to disempower themselves and parliament and give the executive free rein.

EU, therefore, citizens could elect those who determined what treaties we were signed up to. Brexit removed that democratic control over treaty-making.

## Abandoning International Democracy

During the decade 2010–20 successive governments used their foreign policy powers to move the UK in an increasingly anti-democratic direction. The May government, in the words of Anne Applebaum (a former friend of Johnson),

> dropped the old idea that Britain should stand up for democracy around the world with amazing speed.[11]

While the UK was still a member of the EU, the Cameron government used its MEPs to support increasingly autocratic regimes in Poland and Hungary.[12] The May and Johnson governments have consistently supported treaty amendments that allow autocratic states to avoid international law in respect of democratic and human rights.[13] Domestically, the Johnson government whipped its MPs to block an amendment to the Trade Bill which would have outlawed trade with states committing genocide.[14] In its trade negotiations the UK has revived a colonial era mechanism, abandoned by the EU in the first half of the decade, called Investor State Dispute Settlement.[15] This allows international investors to sue democratic authorities in private (and generally secret) courts if they make a decision which affects their investments. Originally designed to allow Western companies to hold on to assets they had acquired through colonialism, ISDS has since been used by multinational corporations to stymie efforts to impose environmental protections and minimum wages and even address crimes committed under apartheid.[16,17]

It's arguable that the Westphalian form of sovereignty may have been acceptable in the nineteenth century, when ordinary people had relatively little interest in foreign affairs. Today, however, global events impact every aspect of our day-to-day lives. As UC Berkeley's Julian Ku and John Yoo put it, globalisation has led to 'economic, social, cultural, and political integration across national borders'.[18]

The trade agreement between the EU and the UK, signed in December 2020, is perhaps the most extreme example of this. Despite MPs not having a vote on the deal, it had an immediate impact on citizens. Exports to the EU (the UK's largest market) fell by nearly half in January 2021. One manufacturer described the new reality as like 'Dante's fifth circle of hell' as he struggled to deal with a massive drop off in sales and mountains of new red tape.[19] Another, whose costs had increased tenfold and left him on the verge of bankruptcy, told the *Guardian*, 'this is what they call sovereignty'.[20]

Since Brexit, 'sovereignty' has increasingly replaced democracy as a guiding principle of foreign policymaking. In reality, there is no practical difference about whether decisions are made in London or Timbuktu so long as those who make them are accountable to those they affect. In pursuit of 'sovereignty' we have given up many of our rights as citizens to influence foreign policy decisions. Since international relations now impact almost every aspect of our lives, this represents a voluntary and substantial step back towards a pre-democratic age.

# 8

# MEDIA BARONS, OLD AND NEW

> *Suppose a commercial broadcaster transmits no polit-*
> *ical debates, interviews or programmes of any kind*
> *(apart from mandatory Party-Political Broadcasts)*
> *in a General Election period. Suppose, also, that*
> *broadcaster then suddenly announces, without*
> *reasons, that it will accord the leader of a major party*
> *three solo prime-time interview slots on each of the*
> *three nights preceding the day of the General Election.*
> *After the event complaint to Ofcom can, it may be*
> *said, procure no effective remedy in such*
> *circumstances.*
>
> > *Davies LJ, R (Liberal Democrats and SNP)*
> > *v ITV [2019] EWHC 3282 (Admin)*

Some cases come along at the perfect time. Some come along on your first day off in three months. *SNP v ITV* was one of the latter. After working on the prorogation case and then the Benn Act case in quick succession, I was looking forward to a week off. Instead, I was instructed by the SNP to challenge ITV's exclusion of Nicola Sturgeon from the first television debate of the

2019 general election. The instructions came from Elaine Motion and Sindi Mules at Balfour and Manson and, holiday or not, I never turn down instructions from Elaine and Sindi. I was led by Philip Coppel QC (my head of chambers). It was to be a case we would lose.

In Chapter 5 we looked at how power is increasingly concentrated in the hands of government. This chapter is about the concentration of power in the hands of a few private individuals. While this may be 'private sector power' rather than 'public sector power', it is no less worrying. The election debates case showed how the laws governing our media allow a small number of individuals to exercise extensive power and answer to no one.

Why is the media a 'constitutional issue'?* Because the media is the lens through which we experience the majority of public discourse. It is how we find out what is going on in the world. To control the media (or even a section of it) is to control what many people (perhaps the majority) believe about the pressing issues of the day. It is to determine who gets a platform. It is to decide how debates are framed, what opinions are aired, and whose faces we grow accustomed to seeing. Democracy only works when we vote based on good information. As the *Guardian*'s Gary Younge put it:

> It is simply not possible to make an informed decision when one is routinely, wilfully and cynically misinformed.[1]

Yet the media is controlled by a small group of powerful people and can be used, with great effect, to manipulate our public

---

* I use the term 'media' to encompass both 'traditional' media (television, newspapers, radio) and social media. Traditional and social media both manifest online and offline.

discourse. An alliance with the media is an essential precondition for success for an elected autocrat.[2] Most importantly, as the election debates case revealed, when the power of the media is misused, there is nothing ordinary people can do about it. Parliament has chosen to frame regulation of the media in such a way as to prevent citizens from holding those who control it accountable in court.

Television debates are a relatively recent addition to UK elections, but the data available indicates that the first debate is the most important. It establishes perceptions of the party leaders and themes which are picked up as the campaigns continue.[3] ITV's first debate was also the only one that took place before postal votes were sent out. There was everything to play for. Shortly before the debate was scheduled, ITV announced that only the leaders of the Labour and Conservative parties would be invited. It had decided that these were the only parties with a chance of forming a government and so didn't think it was worth including the others.

Philip and I were instructed the next morning. We spent the day in his room in chambers (ably assisted by his then pupil, Olivia Davies) poring over the Communications Act and Broadcasting Code, powered by espresso from the machine that Philip keeps sandwiched in his bookshelf between *Information Law* and *Cornerstone on Electoral Law* – both written by him. At the end of the day, we met with Sindi and senior SNP officials. We told them we thought our case arguable. The debate was scheduled for the following Tuesday, so we had to move fast. Over the following eight hours (6 p.m. to 2 a.m.) I drafted our written argument. Over the next seven hours (2 a.m. to 9 a.m.) Philip came up with the final draft. Our clients reviewed the claim in the morning, and we sent out the claim to the court before lunch.

## Traditional Media

*ITV v SNP* was ultimately a case about political power. The parties invited to television debates have a significant electoral advantage. A televised debate offers an unprecedented platform; the opportunity to be inside people's living rooms, to make your case to them and to confront your opponent. The decision as to who benefits from this platform lies in the hands of private individuals and companies. Philip and I sought to put to the court a simple proposition: ITV was performing a public function (hosting the first election debate) and the law required it to exercise that function impartially. Purporting to decide who 'had a chance of being prime minister' (and who did not) before a vote was cast was handing a massive electoral advantage to the Labour and Conservative parties.

In traditional media, power depends substantially on the number of people one can reach with one's message. The greater one's audience, the more one can charge for advertising (economic power) and the more people one can influence (political power).

This is not to say private ownership is inherently problematic. Indeed, from a democratic perspective, it is desirable. The problem lies in monopoly. Whenever monopolies exist, whether controlled by the state or the private sector, power is concentrated in the hands of a few individuals. Debates about media freedom often get bogged down in nineteenth- and twentieth-century experiences, when autocrats sought to extend state control over the press. We still tend to understand press 'freedom' as 'freedom from the state'.[4] However, a 'free' press is one that is free from domination by any party, whether they wear the clothes of the state or the private sector.

British media has always been dominated by a few wealthy

owners. For much of the twentieth century the press was dominated by Lords Beaverbrook and Northcliffe. Beaverbrook built the *Daily Express* into the UK's highest selling newspaper.[5] Northcliffe's empire included *The Times* and the *Daily Mail*. It was so large that, in 1914, it was estimated that he controlled 40% of the morning newspaper circulation, 45% of circulation in the evening and 15% on Sunday.[6] The dominance of Beaverbrook and Northcliffe was, however, offset by an independent press which commanded a substantial audience.[7] Much of this book is about things that have changed in recent years. The problem identified in this chapter is that today's press is no more free than that of the early decades of the twentieth century (at a time when most people weren't allowed to vote). The democratisation of the nation, which leapt forward over the course of the twentieth century, has never extended to traditional media. Our lens on the world thus remains defined by a nineteenth-century balance of power.

Beaverbrook and Northcliffe have been replaced by Rothermere, Murdoch and the Barclay brothers. Lord Rothermere owns the *Daily Mail*, the *Mail on Sunday*, the *Metro*, a number of regional newspapers and substantial shares in ITN (which controls ITV). He is a billionaire who inherited much of his wealth and is 'non-domiciled' for tax purposes, meaning that (officially at least) he cannot be said to live in the UK.[8] He is a high-profile supporter of the Conservative Party. The Barclay brothers own the *Daily Telegraph*, the *Sunday Telegraph* and *Tatler* magazine. They are supporters of the Conservative and UKIP parties and live on the island of Sark, again minimising the tax they are required to pay in the UK. Rupert Murdoch, an American citizen, owns the *Sun*, the *Sun on Sunday*, *The Times*, the *Sunday Times* and a controlling stake in Sky.[9] The *Express*, the *Sunday Express*, the *Daily Star* and the *Daily Star on Sunday* are controlled by Richard Desmond, a Conservative Party donor.[10] The *Independent* and the *Evening Standard* are owned by Evgeny Lebedev (Lebedev's father bought him the *Evening Standard*).[11] He is close to leading figures in government and Boris Johnson made him a life peer in 2020.[12]

Of the remaining major publications, the *Mirror* and the *Sunday Mirror* are owned by a public limited company and the *Guardian* is owned by an independent trust. In 2016 the National Readership Survey recorded that publications controlled by the 'big six' media barons amounted to nearly 75% of the market.[13] Although ownership of television companies is slightly broader (and offset by the BBC, which will be discussed below), it is notable that both Murdoch and Rothermere own substantial stakes in Sky and ITV.

The big six answer to no one. In *SNP v ITV* we sought to rely on the Communications Act. This sets (apparently) strict criteria for ensuring that television companies remain impartial during an election. But the High Court rejected our arguments. Even though the election debates would influence the outcome of the election, the judges said ITV was not exercising a 'public function'. This piece of legal technicality had an important result: citizens were not entitled to challenge ITV's decisions in court, even if it appeared they breached the law. The court went on to decide that the Communications Act (and its associated codes of practice) should only be applied with a light touch. The requirement for 'impartiality' had a broad meaning; it didn't, in effect, mean that all major political parties had to be given a chance to make their case during the election.

The court went on to say that if the SNP had a complaint, the proper course was to take the matter up with Ofcom (the media regulator). In practice, however, this is a waste of time. Ofcom could not have changed ITV's decision in advance of the debate.

It generally only acts after the fact, takes months to reach a decision and, in any case, can only impose fines (which, compared
with the profits made by many media owners, are negligible).
The court did not consider whether Ofcom could act sufficiently
quickly to prevent the harm from a short notice debate (beyond
speculating that it might be capable of doing so). The result of
the judgment is that private sector broadcasters can explicitly
favour one political party over others during a general election
(despite the apparent requirement for impartiality in the
Communications Act). During the hearing Philip raised the
spectre of a broadcaster that makes a last-minute decision to
give the Prime Minister four hours of airtime the day before an
election. In such a circumstance, the court accepted, there
would (in practice) be nothing the opposition parties could do.
Broadcasters thus wield terrific unaccountable power, potentially enough to determine elections. If the extreme abuse of this
power is (so far) hypothetical, the power itself is very real.

Does the media influence the public? Politicians certainly
believe so. One member of David Cameron's Downing Street
team told the journalist Tim Shipman that the decision of the
'big six' to support Brexit was a significant factor in the outcome
of the 2016 referendum. Describing the feeling in Cameron's
'remain' camp, he said 'if the *Mail*, *Sun* and the *Telegraph* had
been for "In" we would have romped home'.[14] Murdoch is a
master at feeding readers his opinions under the guise of non-
news content. The *Sun* famously put talking points from
favoured lobby groups like the Taxpayers Alliance into the
mouths of topless models on Page 3.[15]

Ministers give media owners unprecedented access to the
business of government. After the 1997 election Tony Blair flew
to Australia to visit Rupert Murdoch in order to assure the press
baron that the Blair government would not interfere with his

business interests.[16] Murdoch also enjoyed two 'off the record' meetings with George Osborne, Chancellor of the Exchequer in the Cameron government, shortly after the 2015 general election. There is no record of what was discussed, but the government subsequently cut funding to the BBC, the chief commercial rival to Murdoch's Sky.

It is difficult to quantify the extent to which the media is able to influence the political decision-making of the electorate. An opportunity arose, however, when the *Sun* switched its support from the Conservative Party to the Labour Party between the 1992 and 1997 general elections. In a quantitative study published in the *American Journal of Political Science*, a group from Georgetown and Johns Hopkins universities examined the changing political allegiances of voters during this time. They concluded:

> If, in the 1997 UK election, the *Sun*'s endorsement was in exchange for a friendly regulatory environment for Murdoch, the concession may have bought Blair between 8 and 20% of his 3.9 million-vote margin over the Conservatives.[17]

Since the 1997 election we have seen the explosion of internet journalism and social media. Initial analysis of the 2020 general election, however, indicates that the majority of online news sources (accessed directly and through social media) were manifestations of traditional media.[18] It seems that the traditional 'paper press' and news media have replicated online (although they have now been joined by online-only news sources, like Facebook News – about which more later in this chapter). We may read their words on screens rather than paper, but the power of the media barons remains significant. This would be less problematic, perhaps, if there was any sort of commitment among media barons to reporting the truth. As we saw in Chapter 2, however, much of the media has enthusiastically adopted bullshit discourses.

Politicians have repeatedly turned down opportunities to challenge media barons. After several years of newspaper reports, and the arrest of one of its senior advisors, the Cameron government ordered an inquiry into press regulation in the wake of the phone hacking scandal. The Leveson Inquiry recommended a stronger regulator and changes to the law to incentivise better standards of reporting. Its proposals were never implemented. The media barons were, instead, permitted to set up their own regulator. Although the inquiry remained only half complete, it was cancelled by the May government.[19] Since Leveson, the press has become even more partisan.[20,21] LBC (partly funded by the non-domiciled Michael Tabor) and talkRADIO (owned by Murdoch) have imported US-style 'talk radio' to the UK, providing another platform for extreme commentators to promote their ideas. Although LBC employs some centrist commentators, they are very much the minority. In August 2020 Murdoch and a group of former Conservative Party and UKIP operatives announced plans to launch partisan television channels in the UK.[22] GB News launched in June 2021 and talkTV launched in 2022. Both seek to ape Fox News which, in the US, uses its platform to support the right wing of the Republican Party. The power of traditional media looks set to increase.

## The BBC

The shadow of the BBC loomed over the election debates case. Although it was not technically a party, we all knew the result of our case could have huge implications for the corporation. We are often told that it's OK for most of the media to be controlled by unaccountable cliques because we have the 'impartial' BBC. The national broadcasting service is supposed to be unbiased, acting as a counterweight to the partiality of the private sector media. It's a good idea in theory.

If we had won the case we would have set a precedent, opening the door for the BBC's impartiality to be tested in court. It would have given us a chance to put to bed a long-running (and depressingly evidence-free) political debate. Successive governments and their allies have promoted the idea that the BBC is 'too left wing'. In 2020, for example, the so-called 'Common Sense Group' of Conservative MPs wrote to the Prime Minister urging him to decriminalise licence fee evasion on the basis of the BBC's 'undoubted liberal bias'.[23] When Tim Davie, a former Conservative politician, was appointed Director General of the BBC in 2020, his first public comment was a criticism of his own corporation for being too left wing.[24]

Despite being widely repeated, this accusation is without evidential basis. Indeed, quantitative studies of BBC output repeatedly demonstrate that the BBC favours Conservative politicians over those from other parties and prefers voices from pro-business and right-wing think tanks. In other words, the BBC leans towards the perspectives of the powerful. Researchers at the University of Cardiff studied the BBC's political output between 2007 and 2012 (a period which included both Labour- and Conservative-led governments). They found, unsurprisingly, that the party in government tended to receive more airtime than the opposition. This advantage was, however, significantly greater when the party in government was Conservative. As Prime Minister, Gordon Brown was preferred to David Cameron (then leader of the opposition) by a ratio of less than two to one. Once Cameron became premier, he was given nearly four times the coverage of Ed Miliband.[25] Roughly the same ratios applied to cabinet ministers. Representatives of big business received substantially more airtime than representatives of organised labour on the BBC by a greater ratio than ITV or Channel 4.[26] BBC panel debates have, on average, a two to one bias in favour of right-wing viewpoints.[27] During the 2014 referendum on Scottish independence, the BBC favoured pro-union voices. Professor John Robertson of the University of the West of Scotland found that 'anti-independence' statements outnumbered 'pro-independence' statements by a ratio of three to two.[28]

BBC reporting often frames issues to favour the government's position.[29] In Chapter 2 we saw how the Home Secretary, Priti Patel, sent a series of bullshit tweets accusing 'activist lawyers' of somehow illegitimately blocking a flight deporting immigrants. Rather than correcting the misinformation, the *Today* programme (the BBC's flagship current affairs radio programme) instead hosted a debate about whether the lawyers who represented the refugees had acted wrongly. Given that barristers have an ethical obligation to represent any client, and both international and European human rights law guarantees the right to a fair trial, this framing was transparently absurd. It was, however, directly in line with the government's talking points.

This editorial stance is perhaps unsurprising given that many of the individuals occupying senior positions at the BBC had formerly worked directly for the Conservative Party. Craig Oliver, the former head of BBC TV News, served as David Cameron's director of communications; Robert Gibb, who edited the BBC's political programmes, took on the same role for Theresa May; and Andrew Neil, formerly the corporation's most high-profile political journalist, previously worked for the Conservative Research Department. At the same time as hosting a series of BBC politics programmes, Neil also worked for the Conservative-supporting Barclay brothers. As Mayor of London, Boris Johnson appointed Guto Harri, a BBC political journalist, to head his communications team. Nick Robinson, the BBC's former political editor and host of the *Today* programme, was a former head of the Young Conservatives.[30] Over the last ten years, therefore, a substantial proportion (potentially a majority) of those making editorial decisions about the BBC's politics coverage have recorded Conservative sympathies. This is not necessarily to criticise those individuals or suggest that holding Conservative sympathies is inherently problematic. It is, however, significant that the national broadcaster's politics coverage is substantially determined by individuals who personally favour the governing party. No other party enjoys the same representation in the upper echelons of the BBC.

Why, then, is the BBC criticised as 'left wing'? We cannot see inside the minds of those who make these claims, but we can see the effects of their actions. In the 1990s Joseph Overton, a fellow of the Mackinac Center for Public Policy in Michigan, proposed the theory that came to be known as the 'Overton Window'.[31] Overton posited public discourse as a spectrum. Ideas or positions become increasingly extreme as you reach either end of the spectrum. The 'Overton Window' is the range of ideas or positions that are politically acceptable at any one time. If a nation engages in a particularly left-wing discourse, then the Overton Window will be towards the left of the spectrum. In right-wing societies, the converse will be true. The way to persuade the public of controversial views, said Overton, was to move the window, encouraging citizens to accept ever more radical ideas as 'mainstream'.

Overton's theory explains why a right-wing government would repeatedly cast the right-leaning BBC as 'left wing'. Even the most strident left-wing critics of the BBC would probably agree that it is not so extremely right leaning as publications like the *Daily Mail*. The BBC's bias is, at most, noticeable but marginal. If one casts balance (or even a slight right-wing bias) as 'left-wing bias', then leaning to the right becomes the new centre ground. The Overton Window moves rightwards. If the public can be persuaded that anything other than full-throated support for the government is 'left-wing bias' then it becomes increasingly difficult for Conservative governments to be challenged or for opposition parties to compete with the government at election time.

Had we prevailed in the elections debate case then the government's claims about BBC bias could have been tested in court, subjected to forensic and evidence-based examination and (likely) proven false. When we lost, the BBC indirectly became further insulated from accountability to ordinary citizens and the government retained its free hand to make unsubstantiated (but politically convenient) claims of 'left-wing' bias. The result is that the public perception of the BBC remains mired in bullshit. While the corporation continues to privilege government viewpoints, more and more people are likely to believe it is doing the opposite. A discourse in which criticism of the government is dismissed as 'bias' is concerning for a democracy.

## Social Media

It may seem that this chapter is missing some important points because it doesn't deal with the question of social media. The reason is simple: it did not arise in the election debates case and has not arisen in any other case that I, personally, have dealt with. That is not to suggest that social media is inconsequential in terms of the issues discussed in this chapter. Indeed, similar concentrations of power exist in social media and they may have a similarly deleterious effect on our constitution. Facebook, Instagram, YouTube and WhatsApp are all owned by the same company in which a single man, Mark Zuckerberg, owns a controlling interest.[32] Twitter is a publicly listed company, but the Chairman, Jack Dorsey, exercises substantial control.[33] The fora in which the majority of social media communications occur are, therefore, substantially controlled by just two men.

Dorsey and Zuckerberg have deliberately elected to structure their platforms in a manner that makes it more difficult for us to make rational decisions about the world around us. Everything we see on social media is determined by algorithms. These rarely distinguish between information which is accurate or inaccurate and often direct users to ever more extreme content.[34] At the same time, social media creates a forum which is largely free of personal accountability. We can use pseudonyms or anonymous accounts to say the sort of things we can never say in person. We can often defame, threaten, lie and abuse with impunity.[35] Whether Zuckerberg and Dorsey et al. deliberately seek to radicalise (which seems unlikely) or have structured their algorithms in that way because there are other commercial benefits (more likely), the effect remains the same.

Social media platforms can be used by powerful actors to influence the democratic discourse.[36] Russia has increasingly sought to influence the internal politics of other states.[37] We don't know the extent of Russia's interference in the UK because, as the Russia Report revealed, the May and Johnson governments declined to investigate the issue from 2016.[38] Similarly, non-state actors can also use money and power to manipulate citizens through social media. During the 2016 referendum both Vote Leave and Leave.EU, the two largest 'leave' campaigns, unlawfully used hundreds of thousands of individuals' personal data to send targeted (and often misleading) adverts through social media and messaging services.[39] Both faced minimal consequences for their actions (indeed several of the people involved were given senior government jobs).

Much of this chapter has been about how the powerful manipulate the electorate. This might, perhaps, appear condescending. It's not. I have been a victim of social media targeting and media misinformation. During the referendum on whether to replace the first past the post voting system with an 'alternative vote' in 2011 I saw an advert which claimed that the cost of moving to AV would mean that less money was available for the NHS. It was, in retrospect, transparently absurd. Nevertheless, the advert confirmed my own cognitive bias and pulled me towards a political position with which I was flirting but had not yet fully adopted. I voted against AV at the referendum. It is a decision I regret to this day. I'm sure many people smarter than me saw through that advert, but I didn't. Our current media works to concentrate power in the hands of a few individuals who answer to no one. And that works against our interests.

# 9

# POPULISM: WEAPONISED BULLSHIT

When I was a pupil barrister, I met a woman in a county court waiting room. What began as a fairly standard interaction quickly became a disturbing lesson on the real-world impact of bullshit discourses. She also threatened to stab me.

This woman had been forced into poverty by government policies (themselves justified by bullshit discourses). But she didn't lash out against the government. Instead, she directed her anger at a family of 'immigrants' (actually just British people with different coloured skin to her). She exemplified how bullshit discourses have been weaponised by those in power to prevent us from making rational decisions as citizens.

County court waiting rooms are small and always cramped. Ten years of cuts have left us without enough judges or courtrooms to deal with cases efficiently. The irony of legal aid cuts is that now many people can't afford lawyers: they must present their cases themselves without knowledge of the law or procedure. As a result, everything takes more than twice as long. It's not unusual to arrive for a case listed at 9.30 a.m. and not be heard until the late afternoon. I try to use the extra time to reach an agreement with the other party.

There are never enough conference rooms. When you have several cases on a list, you end up shuttling between parties sat in different parts of the waiting room. You can speak in a low voice, hide behind a folder or huddle in a corner but, ultimately, most other people in the room will hear your conversation.

I had three cases on a 2 p.m. list. All involved social housing tenants who were behind with their rent. I represented the landlord (a housing charity) and was instructed to either ensure the rent was paid or else an order was made for eviction. The first case passed off relatively smoothly. The second and third were more challenging. One involved a family of Indian descent. The parents were jobless and receiving Universal Credit. For some reason their UC payments had been stopped and they had, consequently, fallen into arrears. They had brought several shopping bags full of papers to court. The duty solicitor and I spent a good half hour sitting on the floor of the waiting room putting them into some sort of order. We both agreed that the benefit cut appeared to be a mistake. It was obviously not reasonable to make a possession order, so I agreed to seek an adjournment to give UC time to correct its error.

The third case involved a single white woman in her thirties, who had recently lost her job. She had, however, some small savings. This meant that she was not entitled to housing benefit at a level sufficient to cover all of her rent. Her arrears had accrued because she had simply not paid the difference. I suggested that she agreed to pay the difference and £1.75 per week towards the arrears, and in return I'd ask the court to adjourn the case rather than make a possession order. She refused. She had overheard me talking to the family from the second case. Why, she asked, couldn't she have the same deal? I explained that they were entitled to benefits which would cover their arrears completely. She didn't believe me. She thought it was because they were 'immigrants'. They weren't. But this didn't stop her screaming that she would kill us both with a knife.

This is the impact of bullshit. The woman saw what she had been taught to see: the 'liberal elite' (the court) giving special treatment to 'immigrants' (the very much not immigrant couple in the waiting room). This pernicious form of bullshit is often called populism.

Populism, broadly put, claims to pit 'the people' against 'the elite'. It has spawned its own cottage industry of academic and media analysis, with hundreds of 'experts' pawing over the question of 'how to respond' to populism. One of the most prominent, the University of Kent's Matthew Goodwin, describes the supporters of populism as seeking:

> To reassert cherished and rooted national identities over rootless and diffuse transnational ones; to reassert the importance of stability and conformity over the never-ending and disruptive instability that flows from globalisation and rapid ethnic change; and to reassert the will of the people over those of elitist liberal democrats who appear increasingly detached from the life experiences and outlooks of the average citizen.[1]

In practice the term 'populism' (at least in today's Britain) seems to describe a loose collection of racist, anti-LGBTQ and authoritarian shibboleths. Brexit was a populist moment. Eighty-one per cent of Brexit voters believed multiculturalism (in practice, different cultures living side by side in mutual respect) to be a force for ill, 80% opposed 'social liberalism' (i.e. support for LGBTQ people, civil and political rights, tolerance of new ideas), 74% opposed feminism, 80% opposed the green movement, 69% opposed 'globalisation' and 80% believed immigration to be a bad thing.[2] Most supported the death penalty.[3]

Politicians and commentators on both the left and the right have bought into the idea of 'populism', leading to much hand-wringing over how the Labour Party can 'win back' populist voters. The 'populism' discourse undoubtedly touches on some real issues. Economic deprivation is a genuine problem. The woman in the court waiting room was clearly suffering real poverty. Yet there is no indication that 'populism' actually has any solutions. Indeed, her populist hatred of 'immigrants' led the woman to threaten to stab the one person trying to help her (me!).

The overwhelming political beneficiaries of 'populism' are authoritarian governments. Our current executive, on any reasonable view, epitomises the 'establishment' or 'elite' that populists claim to stand against. They are overwhelmingly the products of public school education, inherited wealth and immense privilege. The key roles in Downing Street were filled with metropolitan political activists. Dominic Cummings (the Prime Minister's senior advisor between 2019 and 2020) is the nephew of a Court of Appeal judge and married into the ducal Wakefield family. When Cummings was forced out of Downing Street in November 2020, Dan Wootton, then executive editor of the *Sun*, commented:

> How sad that there's not a place for a genuinely revolutionary outsider like Dominic Cummings in government. The liberal media and the establishment got him in the end. He has so much left to do.[4]

Wootton's tweet seeks to portray a rich, powerful, privileged white man as somehow marginalised. Cummings is a quasi-aristocrat who spent much of his career working in Westminster.[5] His major political contributions were running the referendum campaigns against electoral reform in 2011 and in favour of Brexit in 2016.[6] On both occasions, Cummings campaigned for a result that overwhelmingly benefitted the party in power at the time. Cummings' downfall had nothing to do with the 'liberal media'. He was forced out after an internal Conservative Party feud.[7] (It was, at least, accurate to describe him as brought down by the 'establishment'.)

Beyond the electoral winners, 'populism' discourse has rewarded commentators like Nigel Farage (a public school educated former stockbroker) with media careers. It has certainly not resulted in an increase in representation for anyone suffering real economic hardship. Even supposedly 'working class' populist voices like Jordan James (who founded the 'Politicalite' blog) and Stephen Yaxley-Lennon (better known as 'Tommy Robinson') were funded by billionaire donors like Robert Mercer, an American hedge fund manager and investor.[8]

'Populism' then, is a typical bullshit discourse: a rallying cry for 'the people' against 'the establishment' which, in fact, only benefits the most powerful. I see the victims of populism in court every day, like the woman in the waiting room. They have been let down by a system in which it is almost impossible for them to succeed yet, buying into populist bullshit, they blame those like them rather than the leaders responsible. Populism exemplifies the impact of bullshit on democracy: leaders can act with impunity because citizens don't have enough of a grasp on reality to make them answer for their errors.

## Making People Poor

The woman in the waiting room was a victim. She had been impoverished by government policy, which was justified by a misleading economic discourse. Populism is rooted in relative economic deprivation. Recent generations, whose parents were able to live comfortable lifestyles on their earnings from working-class jobs, find themselves living increasingly precarious lives. It's entirely understandable that people in this situation look for someone to blame. Populism encourages them to blame immigrants, women, the 'metropolitan elite', gays, trans people and the political left for their problems.[9] This is where populism becomes more complex than other varieties of bullshit. The economic conditions for it to occur were, themselves, created by those who benefit most from populism. Populism is like a bullshit onion: the more one examines it, the more layers of bullshit one finds.

Poverty is not an unfortunate coincidence or the tragically inevitable result of ineffable forces. It is the result of deliberate choices by governments, decisions to economically disempower the majority of people.[10]

Phoney capitalism created the conditions which impoverished the woman in the waiting room. The Cameron coalition's austerity programme cut social security by £37 billion over the course of the decade and rolled back public services, local authority budgets and the NHS.[11] The flagship 'Universal Credit' reduced the sums paid to individuals while adding to the cost of internal bureaucracy.[12] Indeed, but for failures in welfare policy, the woman in the waiting room would likely have been entitled to sufficient housing benefit and would never have been at court at all. It may be entirely coincidental that in 2009 the Conservative Party published research showing that recipients of social security were more likely to vote Labour.[13] Of the fifty councils which suffered the most severe effects of austerity, thirty-eight had a Labour majority. On average, the spending power of Labour councils was reduced by 34%, compared to 24% for Conservative councils.[14]

Since the 1980s governments have consistently restricted the right of citizens to advocate for jobs or better pay and conditions in the workplace. The Thatcher government passed no fewer than six Acts of Parliament dictating what trade unions can and can't do and used the national security apparatus to infiltrate and undermine unions and intimidate members.[15] The Cameron government effectively outlawed most strikes,[16] and restricted unions (along with charities) from involvement in politics.[17] No such restrictions were placed on sectors (such as think tanks or lobbyists) which generally support the government.[18] It's no surprise that, since the 1980s, real wages have fallen consistently. Since 2010 the UK has experienced the slowest real wage growth since records began.[19] Meanwhile rents have increased by some of the largest margins on record.[20] Thirty years ago, the woman in the waiting room would likely have been able to afford her rent even in a low paying job. By the time I met her, that was increasingly difficult.

Philip Alston, the United Nations Special Rapporteur for Poverty, found that the impacts of austerity have fallen most heavily on the least powerful.[21] Many families on low incomes are unable to afford food. Food bank usage reached its highest level on record during the last decade.[22] Household debt, for those on lower incomes, has risen dramatically. In 2012 the Bank of England found that 14% of households spent more than a quarter of their income on debt repayment. For the poorest 10%, that figure rose to 47%.[23] The austerity policies stunted economic growth leading to the longest period of wage stagnation since the Napoleonic wars.[24] Although the rate of employment increased between 2010 and 2019, much of the growth was in the 'gig economy' on part-time, 'zero hours' or temporary contracts.[25]

The number of people sleeping rough doubled between 2010 and 2016. In 2016 alone homelessness rose by 16%, while 123,000 were homeless in 2020.[26] This is not an accident. It is the predictable (and predicted) result of decisions taken by successive governments in full view of the facts. During the 1980s the Thatcher government's 'right to buy' policy forced local authorities to sell off housing stock at below market price. In 2016 the Cameron government forced independent housing associations to do the same. Governments provided preferential mortgage rates for private landlords, allowing them to buy up housing stock sold under 'right to buy' and rent it out at far higher rates than the local authorities or housing associations had done. At the same time governments, through policies like 'help to buy', incentivised house purchase but not house building, driving up house prices and, consequently, rents. Home seekers, therefore, face an ever more vicious competition for housing. Regulation of the quality of housing is light touch and enforced by local authorities which are increasingly starved of funds. Much of the housing provided is of low quality. Rather than address the structural issues making people homeless, governments have given a further subsidy to private landlords in the form of housing benefit.[27]

Predictably, private landlords enjoy vast amounts of economic privilege as a result of these policies. The Citizens Advice Bureau estimates that private landlords make as much as £5.6 billion per year from properties that don't meet legal minimum standards, and £1.3 billion of this is provided by the state through housing benefit. One landlord, Richard Benyon (who also happens to sit in the House of Lords), obtained (through his company)

£625,000 in just one year from housing benefit payments.[28] This, in turn, increases the pressure on social landlords (like my client). More people need homes but high property prices mean these landlords can't afford to expand their housing stock. Social landlords are forced to increase the rents on their current properties so they can afford the necessary expansion.

Housing activists often paint landlords as the villain of this piece. I disagree. Landlords, like any other businesspeople, are entitled to take the economic opportunities on offer (some of those who are companies or trusts have a legal obligation to do so).[29] I have no objection to acting for landlords (indeed, I have an ethical obligation to do so under the 'cab rank' rule). The issue is not one of private morality but public policy. Perhaps some private landlords would have amassed similarly large profits in a genuinely competitive market. We will never know. The fact is that the profits amassed in the private rental market were achieved with substantial state assistance. When government 'picks a winner', as it did with private landlords, then the market is not competitive and not free.

Both the fact of economic deprivation and the bullshit notion that it occurred under 'free market' circumstances create the conditions in which populism flourishes. As one group of researchers put it:

> [Populist politicians flourish when] Poor economic performance, which manifests itself in slow or no growth, feeds dissatisfaction with the status quo. It fosters support for populist alternatives when that poor performance occurs on the watch of mainstream parties. Rising inequality augments the ranks of those left behind, fanning dissatisfaction with economic management. Declining social mobility and an absence of alternatives reinforce the sense of hopelessness and exclusion.[30]

The economic challenges faced by the least powerful are, of course, not all the result of government interference. The economic alienation of many is a function of long-term economic change (and occurred under both Conservative and Labour governments). Globalisation, for example, has caused (among other things) manufacturing jobs to be relocated abroad, leaving a dearth of well-paid and secure working-class jobs. By legislating to restrict union activity, however, governments have restricted the ability of citizens to lobby for state action to address these issues. The austerity agenda, meanwhile, removed the social safety net.

Voters in the most economically deprived areas (with the exception of cosmopolitan cities like London and Manchester, which are discussed below) were more likely to vote for Brexit (a project helmed and funded, for most of its life, almost exclusively by privileged white men) and, since 2019, are more likely to vote Conservative. The economically alienated thus often vote in large numbers for the very people that disenfranchised them. Why? Because 'populist' politicians and commentators have convinced voters to blame vulnerable groups like immigrants or the unemployed.[31] Populism is not so much facing up to an 'uncomfortable reality' as it is a giant con.

## Blame the Immigrants

As recently as the early 1990s very few of us thought immigration was an important issue.[32] From the mid-1990s, however, the tabloid press saturated the public with (often bullshit) coverage of immigration 'issues'. Between January 2000 and January 2006, for example, the *Sun*, *Daily Mail* and *Daily Express* (and their Sunday counterparts) mentioned the phrase 'asylum seeker' in 8,163 articles. This amounts to just under four per day.

Articles broadly riffed on the theme of the 'threat' posed by asylum seekers. They implied a large number of asylum seekers and immigrants were settling in the UK every year, that they represented some sort of danger to British people and they received special treatment (there is no compelling evidence to support any of this).[33] By the mid-2000s, somewhat unsurprisingly, more than 36% of us thought immigration was an important issue. It has remained in the 'top ten' most important issues to the British public ever since.[34] In the Brexit referendum, opposition to immigration was one of the few issues that genuinely united 'leave' voters.[35]

Much of what Britons believe about immigration is bullshit. Migrants from Europe make a net contribution to the UK economy.[36] Uneven population and income distribution means that, in some places, immigrants will require more support from public services or appear to be in competition for jobs. But anti-immigration sentiment is actually highest in areas of low or no immigration.[37]

It is not people's experience of immigration that drives anti-immigrant sentiment but their perception. This is the essence of the invented enemy bullshit. Those who experience the reality of living side by side with immigrants are less likely to see them as an 'enemy'. Those who (like the woman in the waiting room) are disconnected from the reality are more likely to buy the bullshit, blaming immigrants for their troubles rather than the politicians who caused them.

## Populism and the Constitution

The effects of populism go well beyond one woman threatening me in a waiting room. They reach right into the heart of our constitution. Populism erodes public faith in (and allows the powerful to justify ignoring) the norms and values that safe-guard our democracy. In Chapter 5 we saw how the executive uses the claim that it alone represents 'the people' to sideline parliament. Populism also creates a perpetual state of national conflict which governments use to justify ever more extreme sanctions against their political opponents and increasing concentration of power in the hands of the executive.[38]

Populism, in many ways, encapsulates all four themes of this book. It is based on many layers of bullshit: a 'movement of the people' which primarily benefits the elite and, in fact, facilitates making the government less accountable to the electorate. The assaults on parliament and the law, discussed in chapters 3 and 4, were justified by populist rhetoric ('Enemies of the people'). The executive's case for its increasing centralisation of power is based on its claim to embody 'the people'. Populism provides an engine for disenfranchisement and socially marginalising anyone who fails to support the government.

Yet populism also comes back to us as citizens. We have, of course, been left vulnerable to the 'populist temptation' through economic failure, education and media saturation.[39] But at some point we have to make a choice as individuals. We choose to blame immigrants for our economic problems. We choose not to question the rich white men who told us to blame the most vulnerable for our problems. We choose to ignore the wealth of information available to us that would reveal the populist bullshit onion for what it is. The woman in the waiting room had been let down by many people but, ultimately, she chose to blame the 'immigrant' family in the corner rather than accept my offer of help.

# 10

# CRUSHING DISSENT

*The right to peaceful protest is an historic, integral part of our democracy.*
    All-Party Parliamentary Group for Democracy
    and the Constitution, Police Power and the
    Right to Peaceful Protest (HC/HL 2019–21)

On 3 March 2021 Sarah Everard was walking home from Clapham Common to Brixton Hill but she never made it home. She was kidnapped and murdered. On 28 February 2021 a man allegedly exposed himself in a fast food restaurant in Kent. Police were called but do not appear to have investigated the matter fully. Both incidents involved the same man, Wayne Couzens, a serving officer in the Metropolitan Police.

In the aftermath of Sarah's murder, police officers advised women in south London to stay at home to avoid becoming victims of assault. Angered that women were, once again, being made responsible for men's violence and full of grief at Sarah's death, a group of women calling themselves 'Reclaim These Streets' (RTS) organised a vigil on Clapham Common to take place on 13 March. RTS boasted a wealth of event-organising experience. They arranged for a socially distanced event (with

PPE), marshals to maintain social distancing, first aiders and a sound system to ensure that everyone could hear without crowding together. They contacted the police and Lambeth Council in advance of the vigil to inform them of their plans.

Initially the Met seemed receptive, arranging a meeting and promising to get back in touch once they had settled on a policing plan. Later that day, however, officers told RTS that 'an organised event with a set time and location would be in breach of the All Tiers Regulations [the lockdown regulations in place at the time]' and 'their hands were tied'. They gave RTS a letter threatening to prosecute them, not only under the lockdown regulations but also under legislation designed for the prosecution of organised crime. RTS faced fines of up to £10,000 and even custodial sentences.

But the Met had got it wrong. The lockdown regulations didn't tie their hands. Gatherings were permitted where those present had a 'reasonable excuse' and the regulations couldn't trump the Human Rights Act, which guarantees the right to protest. The Met's duty was to consider, carefully, whether banning the event was proportionate (i.e. there had to be no way the risk of coronavirus transmission could be mitigated without banning the event). RTS knew this and so began proceedings for an emergency judicial review. On 12 March, at the 'door of the court', the Met changed its mind and accepted RTS's interpretation of the law. Mr Justice Holgate, nevertheless, reminded both parties of the effect of the Human Rights Act and the lockdown regulations and sent them on their way, adding 'it may well be that there will be further communications between the claimants . . . and the police . . .'[1]

Justice Holgate was right. With the legal position clarified, RTS and the Met held another meeting. Halfway through, and without notifying RTS, the Met released a public statement claiming that the court had ruled in its favour (technically correct but only because it reversed its position) and the vigil was banned. With the threat of prosecution hanging over them, RTS withdrew from organising the vigil. Nevertheless people (including the Duchess of Cambridge) gathered on Clapham Common throughout the following day. The Met adopted a policing plan, Operation Pima, which assumed the lockdown regulations totally banned all protest. Officers on the scene ordered those present to disperse. At around half past six officers forced their way through the crowd, formed a cordon around the bandstand (from which some people were making speeches) and arrested the speakers. Women in attendance were pushed and shoved and the tributes laid to Sarah Everard were trampled underfoot.

While all of this was going on the government introduced the Police, Crime, Sentencing and Courts (PCSC) Bill to parliament. The Bill, as we shall see later in the chapter, dramatically expanded the power of the police to ban peaceful protests. This provoked a number of protests! In Bristol, a protest turned violent after police used pepper spray and dogs to break it up. Over the next week police repeatedly broke up peaceful protests and violent clashes ensued. More than sixty protestors and forty police officers were injured.

Since January Geraint Davies and I had been working alongside Lord Garnier QC (a former Solicitor General), Daisy Cooper, John Nicolson and Dawn Butler to set up the All-Party Parliamentary Group on Democracy and the Constitution. The APPG is a forum for parliamentarians to investigate constitutional issues. At its first meeting, the APPG launched an inquiry into the events at Clapham and Bristol. Jonathan Djanogly (a former Shadow Solicitor General) and Lord Hendy QC joined, and I was appointed inquiry counsel. Together we began investigating the police's behaviour.

This chapter brings us back to enfranchisement. Dissent is essential to democracy and the right to protest has been enshrined in our constitution for at least two centuries. In 1819, after the Peterloo Massacre, the London Court of Common Council recognised 'the undoubted right of Englishmen to assemble together for the purpose of deliberating upon public grievances'.[2] A century and a half later, Lord Denning explained:

> The right to demonstrate and the right to protest on matters of public concern . . . are rights which it is in the public interest that individuals should possess; and, indeed, that they should exercise without impediment so long as no wrongful act is done. It is often the only means by which grievances can be brought to the knowledge of those in authority – at any rate with such impact as to gain a remedy. Our history is full of warnings against the suppression of these rights . . . As long as all is done peaceably and in good order, without threats or incitement to violence or obstruction to traffic, it is not prohibited.[3]

The right to protest is also protected by articles 10 and 11 of the European Convention on Human Rights (given effect in domestic law by the Human Rights Act), the International Covenant on Civil and Political Rights, and the UN Human Rights Committee's 'General Comment 37'.[4]

Governments, and police in particular, have always had a problematic relationship with dissent. Since 2010 things have got much worse. Successive governments and parliamentary majorities have used their powers to outlaw various forms of dissent. The latest and perhaps most egregious step is the PCSC Bill.

## The PCSC Bill

The Bill massively expands the powers available to police to place conditions on and, should they so choose, ban peaceful protests. Previously police could only impose conditions where they were satisfied that the event would cause 'serious damage to property, serious disruption, or incite unlawful behaviour'.[5] The Bill empowers police to condition protests where they cause 'serious unease', too much noise or have a 'significant impact'. None of these terms are defined and the Bill empowers the Home Secretary to change their meaning almost at will.[6] Given that the point of protest is to have a 'significant impact', the Bill effectively gives police the power to ban any protest they choose. For example, standing outside a high street chain informing people that it benefits from child labour could be banned if someone, on the basis of that information, might decide not to go into the shop.

The Bill also expands the offence of public nuisance so that it includes anyone believed to have caused 'serious annoyance'. As a direct response to the Black Lives Matter protests, the Bill raises the maximum sentence for damage to a statue to ten years.[7] To put that in perspective, the maximum penalty for racially aggravated actual bodily harm is seven years: you can now go to prison for longer for protesting against racism than for committing racist assaults.

## Politicising the Police

Police in a liberal state should be law enforcers and preservers, not lawmakers. Yet parliament increasingly offloads its law-making responsibility onto police. Public order legislation gives police such broadly defined powers that, in practice, they are required to both decide which protests can take place and enforce the decision. Under the various lockdown regulations police were required to determine whether individuals had a 'reasonable excuse' for gathering and, consequently, whether a gathering was lawful. In oral evidence Assistant Commissioner Louisa Rolfe denied this amounted to 'making law'. She argued that it was for individuals to decide for themselves whether they had a 'reasonable excuse'. It was certainly true that an individual with a 'reasonable excuse' could, on receiving a fixed penalty notice under the lockdown regulations, challenge it in court. But the cost of doing so was higher than the fine. Defendants were, in effect, punished more harshly for challenging fines than they were for breaching the regulations in the first place. In any case, individuals who believed they had 'reasonable excuse' could do nothing to prevent police from forcibly clearing them from an area (as they did at Clapham and Bristol).

Even in normal times, the Public Order Act leaves the imposition of conditions almost entirely to the discretion of police. The courts may only intervene after the fact (and then only if the condition is so absurd that 'no reasonable officer' could consider it justified).

In giving them the role of law maker as well as law enforcer, parliament has put the police in an unfair position. As Lord Paddick told the inquiry, when police are seen as objective, they gain authority with the public. Officers enforcing parliament's decision can be seen as just doing their job. When, however, the police are seen as banning a protest themselves, their authority is compromised. It compounds the inevitable antagonism between officers and protestors. At both Clapham and Bristol officers reported 'abusive language' from protestors. When I read the transcripts, I discovered that much of that language was centred around criticising officers for the decision to 'ban' the events.

As the inquiry progressed we took evidence from a number of groups involved in protests other than those at Clapham and Bristol. Paul Stephens, a retired police sergeant and activist with Extinction Rebellion, produced records of police responses to demonstrations (obtained through a freedom of information request). They revealed that the Home Secretary had repeatedly contacted officers to urge them to take more aggressive action.

In one demonstration, at a printing site used by News UK in Hertfordshire, the logs show protestors had locked themselves to gates and other parts of the property, thereby preventing access. The police initially approached the situation relatively cautiously, acknowledging that 'lockons' were dangerous situations and protestors could not be removed safely until sufficient officers were in place. In the event, waiting for such officers to arrive did not pose much of a problem because the printworks would not need to open for several hours. The Home Secretary, however, called 'throughout the night' urging police to remove protestors more quickly, apparently regardless of whether specialist officers were on the scene or whether removals could be accomplished safely.

Whether through being put in the position of lawmaker by parliament or pressured by the executive (or something else), the police now do appear to adopt political positions. Assistant Commissioner Rolfe, in her evidence, stated that the Metropolitan Police does not recognise the full extent of the positive obligations conferred by the right to protest. She claimed that there is 'no obligation' to facilitate protest in UK law and, as a result, the Met only considered itself bound to take positive action to assist protestors in very limited circumstances (such as when they were in danger from violent counter protestors). This differs dramatically from the instructions given by the courts, which go well beyond merely restricting counter protests:

> The authorities have a duty to take appropriate measures with regard to lawful demonstrations in order to ensure their peaceful conduct and the safety of all citizens . . .
>
> In particular, the Court has stressed the importance of taking preventive security measures such as, for example, ensuring the presence of first-aid services at the site of demonstrations, in order to guarantee the smooth conduct of any event, meeting or other gathering, be it political, cultural or of another nature.[8]

It is notable that, at Clapham, the Met's refusal to cooperate with RTS actually prevented first aiders from attending. During the Bristol protests there were reports of first aiders being attacked by officers while they attempted to tend to the injured.[9]

In 2009, in the wake of the death of Ian Tomlinson during protests around the G20 summit, police adopted a 'human rights compliant' framework for public order situations.[10] It prioritised dialogue, communication and commitment to facilitating peaceful protest. That approach has since been largely abandoned.[11]

At Clapham the police appeared to decide that certain forms of peaceful dissent would not be tolerated. The Met's own evidence (given to Her Majesty's Inspectorate of Constabulary and subsequently considered by the APPG) was that the decision to use force was made when the event 'started to feel more like a protest than a vigil'. Assistant Commissioner Rolfe justified the intervention by saying people were 'chanting, shouting speeches, some had placards'. It's notable that those speeches were, in general, critical of the police.

While the APPG investigated the Clapham and Bristol events another inquiry, chaired by Sir John Mitting QC, was investigating police spying on peaceful activist groups. The 'Spy Cops' inquiry (and the reporting in the *Guardian* which uncovered the scandal) revealed infiltration of peaceful groups going back decades. Of the 248 groups revealed to have been infiltrated, only five espoused right-wing politics. The other 243 comprised left-leaning, animal rights and justice campaigns.[12] Paul Stephens gave evidence that the police continue to attempt to infiltrate peaceful activist groups. He told the inquiry that officers had attempted to recruit him as a covert human intelligence source.

## Anti-Dissent Culture

Increasingly, both the police and the government treat those who dissent as an enemy to be vanquished. After the Black Lives Matter protests in summer 2020, the Home Secretary publicly described protestors as 'dreadful'.[13] Within months the government moved to limit teaching about racial inequalities, banned museums from moving or contextualising statues of racist figures from history and attacked the National Trust for researching the links between its own properties and the slave trade.[14]

Witnesses described police in Bristol beating protestors (including journalists and medics) with batons and the edges of shields. In the aftermath of the protests, officers, disguised as postal workers, forced their way into the homes of two different women (one twenty-one years old, the other sixteen) who had allegedly attended the protests. One was handcuffed in a state of undress. Male officers cracked jokes with each other while she had a panic attack. The other was pushed against a wall and threatened with tasers. Neither woman was charged with any offence. Police publicly admitted that they had not drawn any distinction between peaceful and violent protestors when clearing streets and parks during the protests. Witnesses told the APPG that it felt like 'revenge policing'.

In Clapham, police refused to cooperate with the organisers, rejecting every suggested measure for a Covid-safe vigil while refusing to explain under what circumstances they would consider the event acceptable. The APPG found that, in both Bristol and Clapham, the police themselves created the conditions that justified the use of force. In Clapham, Lambeth Council advised the Met that some sort of protest would likely happen even if RTS did not organise it. The choice, therefore, was between an organised event with measures in place and marshals to ensure that the risk of Covid transmission was minimised, and an ad hoc event in which police had no way to liaise with organisers. Police chose the latter option and then used the lack of organisation (such as crowding around the bandstand, caused by lack of a sound system) as a pretext for the use of force to disperse those present. In Bristol police complained that no one would identify themselves as an organiser. It subsequently transpired that they had previously threatened anyone identified as organising a demonstration with fines of up to £10,000.

Beyond the Clapham and Bristol events, we received evidence of police using their broad powers to frustrate peaceful protest. This included publishing the names and home addresses of Extinction Rebellion protestors online (in breach of normal practice), leading to several being harassed, standing by while private security firms trespassed on private land and assaulted protestors (who had the owner's permission to be present), and groping and harassing women attending anti-fracking demonstrations. Indeed, analysis from the University of York suggests that police seek to actively frustrate and suppress anti-fracking protests.[15]

## What Happens when the Police get it Wrong?

All public authorities get things wrong and all public authorities are criticised. Errors are inevitable; what matters is how you correct them. One of the benefits of democracy is that we can improve the performance of our public institutions by pointing out where they have gone wrong and how they can do better. Yet criticism of public authorities like the police is increasingly not tolerated. In the aftermath of the Clapham Common violence, the Commissioner of the Metropolitan Police, Cressida Dick, made a public statement essentially claiming no one had the right to criticise the Met:

> They have to make these really difficult calls and I don't think anybody should be sitting back in an armchair and saying, 'Well, that was done badly' or 'I would've done it differently' without actually understanding what was going through their minds.[16]

Commissioner Dick's career has been riddled with controversy. She was appointed to the role after being officer in command of the operation in which Jean Charles de Menezes, an entirely innocent Brazilian electrician, was shot in the head eleven times after being wrongly identified as an Arab terrorist. Dick said:

> If you ask me whether I think anybody did anything wrong or unreasonable on the operation, I don't think they did.[17]

Dick was cleared of personal wrongdoing but the Met as a whole was found guilty of criminal offences under the Health and

Safety at Work Act. Dick was eventually forced to resign after the Met was accused of failing to properly investigate multiple allegations of lockdown breaches at 10 Downing Street. These were the same laws relied on by the police to suppress the Clapham Common vigil.[18]

Victims of police misconduct are advised to avail themselves of the relevant constabulary's internal complaints procedure. Several witnesses told the APPG that victims rarely have confidence in these processes. As if to illustrate why, Avon and Somerset Constabulary gave evidence claiming that complaints about 'blading' (the use of a riot shield as an offensive weapon by striking a person with the edge) of protestors had been investigated and not upheld. The APPG, however, saw footage of officers blading protestors who were lying or sitting prone on the floor and presenting no threat to officers. The inquiry's verdict was:

> In our view there are instances in which the use of blading during the Bristol events was unjustified, entirely excessive, and may amount to criminal offences against the person.[19]

Left to its own devices, Avon and Somerset Constabulary had considered this behaviour entirely appropriate.

Her Majesty's Inspectorate of Constabulary (HMIC) investigated the Met's conduct at the Clapham vigil. On 30 March it published a report largely exonerating the Met and, extraordinarily, went beyond its terms of reference to attack critics of the Met as 'uninformed' and showing a 'lack of respect'.[20] The APPG reviewed the HMIC report as part of its inquiry. It found:

> While HMICFRS obtained evidence from 'police officers at various levels of seniority, the RTS organisers, politicians and

officials in central and local government', it appears not to have obtained evidence (or not to any significant extent) from any individual who attended to participate in the Clapham Common event. This is, in the APPG's view, a significant failing. While the APPG is aware that the report was produced quickly (and makes appropriate allowance) it is impossible to give the report full weight.[21]

In other words, it's no wonder HMIC exonerated the Met when it didn't speak to any of the victims. During the inquiry the APPG also received worrying evidence about the objectivity of HMIC. Lord Paddick produced reports from a whistle blower inside HMIC. Alice O'Keefe alleged that HMIC had assured the Home Secretary that it would back her plans for the PCSC Act in a forthcoming report, before investigators even began work. Members of the report team, said O'Keefe, compared peaceful protestors to the IRA.[22]

Victims unable to get satisfaction from internal complaints processes or organisations like HMIC have no choice but to go to court. Yet, for most people, this simply isn't an option. As we saw in Chapter 4, the government has removed legal aid for judicial review. It has also largely done so for civil actions against the police. Only those with substantial funds are realistically able to challenge the police in court.

## Dissent isn't Trending

Protest is not the only form of dissent and it's not the only victim of government crackdowns. Since 2010 governments have eliminated or restricted a range of other sources or forms of dissent. The Cameron and May governments cut funding across the higher education sector but eliminated teaching grants for the

humanities entirely. The humanities include political philoso-
phy, history, law and public policy; some of the subjects most
likely to produce criticisms of the government.[23]

Universities are natural centres of free thought. Students'
unions have consistently opposed government higher education policies, regularly bringing together tens of thousands of
students with marches, rallies and online petitions. Student
activism predates, of course, the last decade but the government
crackdown is new. In 2018 the May government established the
Office for Students, with the power to interfere in the governance and decisions of (formerly independent) universities and
student unions. The Adam Smith institute, a think tank with
close links to government, has recommended going further. In
2020 it urged the government to forcibly break up student
groups that campaigned on political issues.[24] The report was
endorsed by the chair of the House of Commons Education
Committee, Robert Halfon, and Sajid Javid, who subsequently
joined the cabinet as Health Secretary.[25]

The arts and culture sector has long given a platform to those
who critique the powerful or hold a mirror up to society. While
everyone has heard of the 'big names' in the arts like the Tate
Modern, the Royal Shakespeare Company or the Royal Albert
Hall, the sector is also a mosaic of large and small organisations
ranging from commercial enterprises packing out thousand-
seat auditoriums to tiny local venues, theatres, galleries and
museums. At its height, in the early years of the twenty-first
century, the sector could claim to reach people of all classes
across the UK.[26]

Between the years 2010–20 the government cut funding to
the arts sector by 43%.[27] Cuts to local authority budgets led to
further cuts amounting to more than £400 million.[28] The
government justified its cuts as part of the 'austerity' drive,

claiming cuts were necessary to 'bring the deficit under control'. As an economic proposition, however, this is nonsensical. The arts are one of the state's most profitable investments. In 2010, for every £1 the government invested it recouped £5 in taxes.[29] Arts and culture is one of the most important facets of the economy. It generates around £77 billion per year (making it a larger economic contributor than agriculture) and employs over 130,000 people.[30] The policy makes perfect sense, however, if the objective is political. Cutting state support for the arts cuts the platform available for those who may criticise the government or the powerful. This is not intended as conspiracy theory. I have no secret evidence that arts cuts are part of a dastardly scheme to thwart democracy. We don't know if silencing critics was the intended effect of successive governments' cuts to the arts budget. We do know, however, that this is what happened. Hundreds of arts organisations, institutions and venues have closed during the last decade.[31] As a matter of fact, therefore, there are now substantially fewer opportunities for artists to criticise the powerful than there were at the start of the decade.

The Cameron government also restricted the activities of independent campaigning organisations that might oppose the government. The Transparency of Lobbying, Non-Party Campaigning and Trade Union Administration Act 2014 restricts charities from spending more than £20,000 campaigning on political issues (which include things like child poverty and healthcare) during an election year. This effectively outlaws campaigns like 'Make Poverty History', in which a coalition of charities and NGOs worked together (primarily in the decade 2000–10) to lobby governments to implement the Millennium Development Goals to reduce poverty in the global south. Unlock Democracy, an NGO, ran a campaign during the 2010 general election for greater regulation of lobbying. Had the

Lobbying Act been in place, that campaign would have been unlawful.[32] Ironically, given its name, the Act leaves most commercial lobbyists entirely unregulated.[33] Trade unions, long the bête noire of governments and a platform for ordinary people to campaign, have been regulated almost into irrelevance snice the late 1970s. The Cameron government restricted political donations from unions and outlawed certain union fundraising for political parties. It may be entirely coincidental that trade unions tend to donate to that administration's political opponents.[34]

All of these decisions provoked different debates. Cuts to the arts were seen as an attack on creativity, university cuts as an attack on education and charity regulation appeared to attack the voluntary sector. Yet the common theme running through all of these is dissent. Universities, unions, charities and the arts all offer a channel through which citizens may criticise the government or learn about ideas of which the government does not approve. All, like the act of protest itself, have been restricted since 2010. British citizens now have fewer opportunities to disagree with those in power than at any point in several decades.

# CONCLUSION: REVITALISING THE CONSTITUTION

*To govern is to choose.*
*Pierre Mendès-France*

I wrote this book to start the conversation about how to reinvigorate our democratic constitution. I don't pretend to have all the answers. Indeed, the only satisfactory solutions will come from a national conversation, not one lawyer's opinion. Given that this book is based only on my own cases and experiences, I have necessarily neglected many important constitutional points and issues. That said, I would like to propose a few targeted constitutional and political reforms to address some of the problems raised in previous chapters and re-orient the constitution back towards the democratic lodestar. Some may, to British ears, sound radical, yet nothing I propose is particularly revolutionary among other democratic states. My proposals should not be taken as a coherent programme for constitutional reform but rather as the start of a much more complex discussion. They can be summarised with three goals: free parliament, restore justice and empower citizens.

## Free Parliament

Parliament must genuinely discharge, rather than merely perform, the duties of the legislature. It may seem strange, given that my experience is primarily legal rather than political, that I start with reforms to parliament instead of the justice system. But the justice system is only as good as the laws that it enforces. The courts, at all times, defer to Acts of Parliament and parliament, at all times, holds the power to reform the courts. We cannot get the legal aspects of our constitution right until we get the political aspects right.

Many discussions of parliamentary reform begin with the House of Lords. It has become axiomatic among democrats that the Lords should be reformed along democratic lines. I don't disagree. An upper house elected, for example, on the basis of proportional representation would add a genuinely national dimension to the representative nature of parliament. This would counter-balance the House of Commons whose members are, at least in theory, bound to their constituencies and therefore required to represent their concerns. It would strengthen the democratic mandate and eliminate one of the most significant hangovers from the pre-democratic constitution. The Lords could be democratised without sacrificing the value it currently brings. If elections were conducted on a list system, parties could ensure those with necessary expertise are all but guaranteed a seat by placing them at the top of their lists. Partisanship could be minimised, and members' minds focused on dispassionate consideration of legislation, by electing members for long terms but prohibiting them from standing for re-election. Fresh blood could be introduced by electing different portions of the house on a rotating basis. Combining an upper house elected on a proportional basis with a lower house elected on the existing first past the post basis would also go a long way towards resolving ongoing debates about electoral reform.

All of the above (and, indeed, many other proposed versions of Lords reform) would represent positive change, but it would not directly target the issues in this book. Therefore, while remaining open-minded (and generally positive) about ideas for democratisation of the Lords, I do not propose them as a panacea for the current parlous state of our constitution. The same is true of questions of devolution. National independence for Scotland, Wales and/or Northern Ireland may be desirable for various reasons but would not necessarily resolve the issues raised in this book and lie beyond its scope.

The challenge faced when considering parliamentary reform is that, in many instances, it is the parliamentary majority itself which has chosen to disempower parliament. MPs must choose to be legislators. Citizens can influence that choice by demanding that MPs step up.

We can't dictate the choices of MPs, but we can reform parliamentary structures and incentives so as to create a framework for better decision-making. Constitutional reform takes time, however. It is likely that, if implemented, many or all of the reforms suggested in the following pages won't appear to work in the short term. Indeed, the argument against almost all of them is that MPs have always been venal and ambitious and always will be. I disagree, but that's not really the point. The aim of the reforms I propose is not to turn inevitably flawed individuals into angels. Rather, it is to remove the institutional impediments to democracy.

The first step is to break the dominance of the executive over parliament. We should begin by giving MPs control over parliamentary business. In 2010 the Cameron government established the Backbench Business Committee, a select committee with the power to suggest debates. Its role, however, is limited. It relates only to a very small percentage of parliamentary business and can be ignored or overruled by the executive. The Business Committee should be chaired by the Speaker and given complete control over the business of the Commons. A similar committee should do the same for the Lords. This would leave legislators to decide for themselves when to scrutinise the government, how long for, what topics to debate, what legislation to consider and for how long. It would end the ability of the executive to avoid scrutiny by denying or limiting the time available to parliament and it would place elected legislators in command of their own business.

Isabel Hardman, in her book *Why We Get the Wrong Politicians*, points out that critics of this proposal

> argue that such a committee would either be a rubber-stamping exercise for what the government wants, if it has an inbuilt majority, or a means by which oppositions could prevent the democratically elected government from getting its way.[1]

I see no problem in the executive occasionally not getting its way in parliament. Indeed, that's what's supposed to happen in an effective democracy. As Lady Hale pointed out in *Miller/Cherry*, the executive has no mandate other than that provided by parliament. Even a directly elected executive would have no better claim to a democratic mandate than the Business Committee itself. Given, as well, that legislation is the business of parliament, not the executive, it is right that the latter should defer to the former on this point. The potential for political shenanigans could be minimised by subjecting the decision of the Business Committee to a vote of the whole house (either by maintaining the current practice of 'programme motions' or on an ad hoc basis).

The danger of the committee becoming a 'rubber stamp' may be remedied by addressing the perverse incentives for MPs. Almost every prospect for career advancement for MPs comes from climbing the ministerial ladder. This allows the executive to exercise substantial (at times, almost complete) control over its MPs. This monopoly of reward must be broken.

First, MPs ought to be paid the same as ministers. There is no 'market rate' for legislators' wages. We make a political decision about how much we think they are worth. The social value of the work done by legislators is no less than that done by members of the executive. Indeed, as the custodians of the democratic mandate, it might be argued that legislators are more valuable. Yet the role of legislator will not be treated as of equal value to that of minister unless it is remunerated at an equal rate. Along with equal pay should come specialist training. New MPs should receive mandatory training in legislative scrutiny and those elected to select committees should receive training in the examination of witnesses.

Second, we should ban MPs from serving in the executive and vice versa within the same parliamentary term. To be a good legislator takes an entirely different skillset from that required to be a good executive. The fact that members of both executive and legislature are drawn from parliament is another historical quirk of the constitution, left over from the days of Walpole and Pitt.[2] It is a relic of a time before constitutional theory and practice had really developed, with no rational justification in the twenty-first century. As matters currently stand, more than one hundred members of parliament are also members of the executive. This means that the executive is largely left to mark its own homework. Any MP who is made a member of the executive must be required to resign their parliamentary seat on the proviso that they cannot stand again until a full parliament has elapsed. This would, in practice, mean they would be required to sit out the next general election. The same rule would apply to a reformed House of Lords. Concurrently, the Prime Minister should be allowed to appoint members of the executive from outside the legislature (although subject to parliamentary confirmation).

One might consider a permanent ban. The system I have proposed is to be preferred, however, because it offers an element of flexibility and the potential for former members of the executive to one day return to parliament to put the experience they gained as ministers to good effect in the legislature. This system would also allow the Prime Minister to appoint ministers with genuine expertise in their brief and, at the same time, eliminate some of the perverse incentives at work among parliamentarians.

Once an MP becomes a minister the next step in their career trajectory is to gain more senior and prestigious ministerial posts. The result is that career-hungry dilettantes bounce from ministry to ministry. They rarely gain the knowledge and experience required to genuinely engage with the public policy issues they face and have little incentive to do so. Indeed, press visibility and party loyalty are generally a more secure path to promotion than genuine competence.[3] The Prime Minister should be able to appoint a top head teacher to the Ministry of Education, a senior soldier to the Ministry of Defence, a healthcare professional to the Department for Health and the country's top economist to run the Treasury. This would reduce the incentive for 'bouncing around' departments. It would, for example, become absurd for a leading diplomat, appointed to the position of Foreign Secretary, to aspire to become Chancellor of the

Exchequer. In the event that a premier simply appointed career-hungry dilettantes from outside parliament, the more independent legislature would be more likely to refuse his or her selections.

My proposal raises the question of whether the executive should be elected separately from the legislature. In view of the issues I have raised in this book, I think it is unnecessary but preferable. It is unnecessary because my proposed system could work on the basis of purely parliamentary elections. When a new party leader wins the general election and is able to form a government, they would resign their seat and appoint their ministers. When the existing Prime Minister's party wins, they would retain their job. It is preferable, however, to elect the executive separately because it gives voters a more genuine choice. The electorate looks for different qualities in the executive and legislature. Voters are asked, when they put a cross in a box on election day, to simultaneously take two entirely different decisions. They must select a local representative for the legislature but also the party (and possibly Prime Minister) they want to form the executive. There is not necessarily any connection between the local candidate's talent for legislation and the governmental competence of the party or its leader. These are two separate questions and voters should be allowed to express themselves on both. The current system all but eliminates that possibility. A directly elected executive (which answers to the legislature) would also add an extra opportunity for citizens to hold power to account. It is likely that, under this system, the leadership of the majority in the legislature and the Chair of the Business Committee would work closely with the executive to bring 'government' bills before parliament.

When similar systems to this have been proposed in the past it has been suggested that they would actually diminish the ability of the legislature to challenge the government. John Bercow, certainly no executive stooge, expressed scepticism:

> I think that the case would have to be made quite strongly as to why it is or how it would be that we would be better served if ministers were not directly and immediately accountable to the House . . . It is a risky enterprise to move away from a situation where, however powerful they might be, they are members of our Parliament and we've got them.[4]

The answer to this critique is that, regardless of whether the executive is drawn from parliament, the legislature must be equipped with the powers it needs to do its job. Parliament already has limited powers to compel ministers to appear before it to answer questions. An independent parliament should retain and extend these powers. Currently, ministers can send someone to answer questions in their place. Anyone who doesn't hold ministerial office (including special advisors, civil servants and media barons) can simply ignore the request. This compares unfavourably with the powers available to even the most insignificant county or magistrates' court. Both civil and criminal courts have the power to summon any witness to appear before them if their evidence is relevant to the matter at hand.[5] Refusal to comply with a summons issued by a court is a criminal offence punishable by a fine or even imprisonment. Parliament can find people 'in contempt of parliament' but the example of Dominic Cummings demonstrates the meaninglessness of such censure.

Parliament must have the power to summon people to appear before it in the same way as a court. Such a power is pointless unless backed up by sanction, so where a witness refuses to comply with a parliamentary summons, parliament must be able to refer the matter to the courts for trial and sentence. It is likely to be impractical for each house, as a whole, to deal with issues like this so the power should generally be exercised in practice by select committees.

Legislators must also be able to access the information required to properly scrutinise bills and/or the actions of the executive. Too often, the executive determines what information parliament and the public will be allowed to see. Parliament must have the power to decide what information it requires and compel its production (again, a power that should be exercisable by select committees on behalf of the whole house). If information really is sensitive then it can be disclosed to the relevant select committee, which will determine for itself which aspects to publish.

Even with the reforms already discussed in place, the executive will be able to avoid scrutiny in substantial areas of public policy by hiding behind the royal prerogative. From a democratic perspective, it is absurd that this relic of a medieval monarchy should continue to exist. It should be abolished. The powers currently exercised under the prerogative should be put on a statutory footing. Parliament should decide how and when prerogative powers can be exercised. Some, like prorogation, should transfer entirely to parliament itself. Others, like foreign policy, should be exercised within a framework set out by parliament. This has two advantages: first, it will mean that the (former) prerogative powers gain a democratic basis; and second, without the fog of legal ambiguity which still surrounds the concept of the prerogative, citizens will, through the courts, be able to ensure that the executive uses its powers lawfully.

These new powers will be of little efficacy if parliament does not have the resources to utilise them effectively. The funds must be available for MPs to hire properly qualified researchers (rather than recent graduates), and for select committees to be supported by qualified advisory and trial counsel who can subject ministers and other witnesses to genuinely forensic questioning on the parliamentarians' behalf.

## Protect Justice

A legislature that is properly equipped to perform its role can turn to reform of the justice system. The goal of the ideas set out below is to empower citizens to hold the executive to account through the courts. This is in the interests of both citizens and the executive. The former would enjoy more genuine and practical protection of their rights while the latter would benefit from more detailed guidance about how to lawfully make public policy.

The objectives of justice reform should be twofold: first, to stop the politicisation and consequent marginalisation of the law; and second, to ensure equal access to justice for all. There is already a law in place which is supposed to stop politicians from making partisan hay out of the justice system. Section 3 of the Constitutional Reform Act 2005 places a duty on all ministers to 'uphold the continued independence of the judiciary'. The Lord Chancellor takes an additional oath of office, undertaking to both 'defend the independence of the judiciary' and 'respect the rule of law'.[6] But these provisions are effectively unenforceable and routinely ignored. When Liz Truss failed to defend judges against attacks in the media after *Miller I* (which, coming before the Supreme Court heard the matter, presented a very real risk of impacting on the independence of the judiciary), or when Robert Buckland endorsed the Internal Market Bill (which explicitly gave the government the power to breach international law), neither was called to answer for breaching their oaths.

The first reform to the justice system, then, must be to impose a genuinely enforceable duty on ministers to both respect and uphold the rule of law and to defend the independence of the judiciary. If the duty is important enough to be enshrined in statute, then it is important enough to be genuinely enforceable. The Constitutional Reform Act must, therefore, be amended to clarify the duty and specify the mechanism of enforcement (judicial review seems appropriate given the administrative court's experience in handling ministerial breaches of statute) and penalties. The latter requires some thought. A fine is often the 'go to' penalty for non-criminal wrongs. In this context, however, it may seem a little disconnected from the nature of the minister's error. A more innovative penalty would be to allow the court, on finding a breach of duty, to refer the minister to parliament, which would then take a straight up or down vote on whether the minister could remain in post. Such a penalty seems more appropriate in respect of an error which, in essence, is linked to the minister's fitness to hold office.

The politicisation of the justice system will not be solved merely by punishing ministers who behave badly. The essential justification for attacks over the last decade has been the claim that judges are interfering in politics. Given that 'politics' can mean almost anything (from shutting down parliament to promising to break the law) this creates an unhelpful ambiguity. The solution is to more clearly define the role of the courts in holding the government responsible. But any attempt to list the acts of the executive that can and cannot be reviewed will ultimately be unsatisfactory. The evolving nature of government means there will always be new issues before the courts. People, including those who serve in government, will always find new and innovative ways to break the law.

A better approach is that taken by the Scots courts. They

determine whether an issue is a proper subject for the courts to consider by reference to the purpose of judicial review.[7] As Lord Drummond Young put it:

> The fundamental purpose of the supervisory jurisdiction is in my opinion to ensure that all government, whether at a national or local level, and all actions by public authorities are carried out in accordance with the law. That purpose is fundamental to the rule of law; public authorities of every sort, from national government downwards, must observe the law. The scope of the supervisory jurisdiction must in my opinion be determined by that fundamental purpose. Consequently, I would have no hesitation in rejecting any arguments based on procedural niceties, or the detailed scope of previous descriptions of the supervisory jurisdiction, if they appear to stand in the way of the proper enforcement of the rule of law.[8]

This is a far more sensible approach, ensuring that the judiciary remains in its constitutional lane while allowing citizens to hold the government to account effectively through the courts.

The three constitutional branches of the state are supposed to balance each other. This falls apart in the face of the 'enabling act' problem identified in Chapter 4. If parliament legislated to give the executive the power to rule autocratically, there may be little anyone could do about it. Many of the attacks on the justice system over the last decade have been executed with the full endorsement of the parliamentary majority. But parliament is elected and judges are not, so it's obviously undesirable to allow the courts to overrule the legislature. How can we address the 'enabling act' problem while staying true to the democratic lodestar of the constitution?

Many favour a written constitution. This would define and

confine the powers of parliament, the executive and the courts to those set out in the constitutional document. I am unconvinced by such proposals for three reasons. First, it is not clear what should be included. Many aspects of the constitution (such as the extent of certain prerogative powers) remain contested, even by the most eminent constitutional scholars. Second, written constitutions tend to choke off all potential for constitutional evolution. The United States is a case in point. The absurd spectacle of supposedly eminent constitutional lawyers, judges and scholars arguing about 'what the founders intended' in the face of twenty-first-century issues is enough to shred the credibility of most arguments for a written constitution. It would be particularly damaging in this country, where our constitution is, in its very essence, evolutionary. Imposing the values and ideas of one generation on our descendants is no recipe for good governance. Third, a written constitution would not necessarily solve the enabling act problem. It might, indeed, exacerbate it. The drafters may use the opportunity of a written constitution to lock in many of the relics of our pre-democratic days that continue to dog constitutional law and politics.

Rather than a full written constitution, I prefer a short, binding statement of constitutional values. These might include, for example, democracy, parliamentary sovereignty, the rule of law, the separation of powers, and human rights (perhaps in cascading order of importance). This would act as a quasi-constitution. Laws made by parliament and the executive (and government actions) must be compatible with the listed constitutional principles.* This would provide a check against a parliamentary majority which attempted to make its own power permanent or sought to chip away at the

---

\* For lawyers: this mechanism essentially expands on and enhances the model provided by the Human Rights Act 1998.

institutions of justice and democracy (such as by limiting judicial review). At the same time, it would maintain sufficient flexibility to allow each generation to interpret the constitution in its own context. It also avoids the problem of whether to enshrine the existing constitution or an improved version. Constitutional principles are already part of our constitutional law but, when expressed as principles rather than rules or laws, they are sufficiently flexible to permit constitutional evolution.

Discussions of the justice system often focus on courts, judges and lawyers. It's easy, therefore, to miss the main actors: citizens. There is little point in justice reform if citizens are not guaranteed access to justice. This means legal aid. Every citizen should have a statutory right to legal advice and, where necessary, representation. This should be a genuine and practical right, not reliant on charity or luck. Where citizens cannot afford advice and representation, therefore, the state must step in. Lawyers should not have to sacrifice their livelihood to do legal aid work so legal aid rates should match the private sector. Lawyers should be chosen for legal aid clients based on their expertise and experience, not whether they are willing to take a pay cut. This isn't about guaranteeing myself a good professional income (although it would be nice . . .); it is about guaranteeing citizens the legal advice and representation befitting their needs. No citizen should have to settle for discount justice. Similarly, the threshold for legal aid should be set at a level to ensure that citizens do not have to sacrifice their financial security before they are offered help. Savings and pensions should not be included in the calculation of eligibility. Citizens should not be punished for good financial decision-making when it comes to enforcing their legal rights.

Can we afford high levels of legal aid? At its absolute height, it represented less than 0.3% of the national budget (a smaller percentage than the cost of writing off unpaid Covid-19 business loans).[9, 10] This seems like a fairly reasonable cost to guarantee a basic constitutional and human right.

## Empower Citizens

One of the key themes of my experience in constitutional law, and hopefully one of the key messages to come out of this book, is that the constitution is more than just our institutions. Civil society is as much a constitutional forum as parliament or the courts and we, as individuals, are constitutional actors of greater importance than ministers or judges. Constitutional reform must, therefore, account for the role of society. Much can be achieved simply by repealing the anti-dissent legislation introduced over the last decade (or, in the case of trade unions, half century). The vast majority of that legislation (such as the Lobbying Act) is almost entirely ineffective at solving the problems it was intended to solve while, at the same time, it imposes deleterious burdens on civil society. There is little to lose and much to gain from consigning it *in toto* to the dustbin of history.

An evolutionary constitution, however, must evolve. We must continue to disperse power as widely as possible or future governments will simply find new ways to abuse it. I propose social reforms under three headings: Truth, Money and Locality.

Beginning with truth: we can't have an effective democratic discourse if most of what we say isn't true. We need to re-ground our public debate in reality. There is a difficult balance to be struck, however. Using the coercive power of the law to force people to tell the truth would inevitably trample on civil rights and thus be equally damaging to our constitution. On the other hand, bullshit is anathema to democracy.

The antidote to bullshit is education. If we, as a society, better understand our constitution, and are better equipped to evaluate what we are told by politicians and the media, then we are less likely to buy bullshit (or spout it ourselves). In school we should educate children with knowledge of the constitution and the skills required for citizenship (like critical thinking, largely eliminated from the National Curriculum by Michael Gove's reforms) in the same way we educate them in English, maths and science. More broadly, politicians must provide better leadership. No one has a better platform to explain constitutional ideas than parliamentarians. Unfortunately, politicians of all stripes often eschew the opportunity to defend liberal principles. There is often little to be gained politically from voicing an unpopular position.

Defending our rights, however, often means plugging away at an unpopular cause. In the nineteenth century those advocating votes for women and working-class men were political pariahs. Not so long ago speaking out in favour of gay marriage was political suicide, until the tides begin to change. Democrats need to be prepared to take the short-term political hits in the name of the longer-term democratic objective. Leadership often means saying things before it is politically convenient to do so.

In any case, short-termist thinking is politically risky. Many politicians seem to believe that if you play the political game, you will eventually get a turn at government. Once there you can begin to fix things. As this book has shown, however, the norms of political combat have changed. Successive majorities have used their dominant position to entrench themselves. Every year the likelihood of those now in opposition getting a turn at power decreases. If politicians want to go back to the old rules, then they need to fight for them. That means not letting attacks on our constitution slide and, more importantly, using them as an opportunity to talk to the public about constitutional and democratic ideas.

Politicians also need to stop bullshitting. One way to reduce (although not eliminate) bullshit is to abolish the ancient ban on MPs calling each other a 'liar' in parliament. If politicians could be called out on their bullshit in our highest-profile democratic forum, then they might be less incentivised to mislead parliament (and, by extension, the electorate). It would also end the farce of politicians being forced to pretend everyone in parliament is a sort of medieval nobleman bound by the rules of chivalry and incapable of telling a lie. Quite obviously, they are not.

Turning now to money: as things currently stand those with more cash simply have a much greater political influence than those with less. It has always been so. This book isn't meant as a critique of capitalism. If you work hard and make money you should be able to enjoy the rewards that brings. Those rewards should not, however, include a greater say in how the country is governed. That is not to say that political donations should be banned. There is an argument that the right to donate to the cause of your choice is an important component of your free-dom of expression. A simple way to put that principle into prac-tice would be to limit donations to political parties to the amount that someone receiving benefits would be able to afford. Everyone would be free to donate but you wouldn't be able to buy more 'freedom of expression' just because you were rich. This would certainly hit the finances of political parties but, where necessary, we may explore the possibility of extending public funding. It might also be argued that parties don't need to spend as much as they do on elections. Is a billboard with a cartoon of Ed Miliband in Alex Salmond's pocket, or an entire consultancy dedicated to making insulting memes, really a necessary use of campaign money? Perhaps if political parties had less money to spend on campaigns they would be required to focus more on free platforms, such as public meetings or television debates, which (at least in theory) require politicians to engage more substantively with the issues.

One area of politics that requires more money is parliamentary candidates. Currently, candidates are required to fund all of their own living expenses while they campaign. This means they must either fit campaigning around work or else take substantial unpaid leave. Those who are already very wealthy have a huge advantage and people on low incomes are largely excluded from standing for parliament. A quick fix would be to provide a publicly funded salary to all those who meet basic criteria (such as being selected as a candidate by a political party with a certain level of membership). This wouldn't solve the class divide in politics, but it would, at the very least, lower some of the barriers to ordinary people seeking to represent their fellow citizens.

Finally, locality: government is more responsive, and citizens are more able to involve themselves in the decisions that affect their lives, when it is local. During the Brexit campaign the EU was often described as a centralising force, sucking power into Brussels. Ironically, the real constitutional centrifuge is not Brussels but Westminster, with ministers and civil servants clawing ever more power from devolved and local governments. The EU, by contrast, enshrines subsidiarity into its constitutional treaties. Subsidiarity means that every decision should be taken at the most local possible level. The same principle should be embedded in UK law (potentially in the statement of constitutional principles proposed earlier in this chapter). Every aspect of government that can be conducted at local level should be conducted at local level; this includes raising the necessary revenue. Local decisions should be taken by local government, answering to local people. This will both make it easier for citizens to engage in the democratic process and make government more accountable to the governed. It may even free up some valuable real estate in Whitehall . . .

It's all very well for me to suggest a bunch of reforms at the end of a book. Lawyers, judges, politicians and civil servants are all just cogs in the constitutional machine. The essential actor is the citizen and the essential action is choice. Citizens made our constitution and will decide whether it continues to evolve with democracy as its lodestar. Much of this book has been about how the powerful have made themselves more so. How they have reversed the dispersal of power that occurred over the course of the centuries and closed off avenues of accountability. Yet all of this ultimately comes down to choices made by citizens. Many of the attacks on our constitution over the last decade have been conducted with the support of the democratically elected parliamentary majority. Government and tabloid condemnations of 'activist lawyers' and 'enemies of the people' obtain substantial public support. We have, to a notable extent, chosen to show contempt for our constitution.

We are now at the point where we need to make another choice: do we still want to live in a democracy? How important is it to us and what are we prepared to do to secure it? Citizenship brings rights but it also brings responsibilities. We must choose wisely.

# ACKNOWLEDGEMENTS

I'm hugely fortunate to have had the opportunity to write this book. Its existence is due far more to good fortune and the kindness of others than anything on my part. This applies both to the fact that I was in a position to write a book like this and also to my journey to becoming a barrister and arguing the cases on which it is based. While I would like to think that hard work on my part played a small role, I am, in truth, mainly the product of the opportunities provided to me by others. I owe an insurmountable debt of gratitude to so many people that I would need an entire other book to address them all, but the following, in particular, stand out.

My parents sacrificed so much to pay for extracurricular activities and university, and top up my scholarships during (oh so many) years of postgraduate study. They coached me through the subjects I struggled with at school (maths!) and instilled in me the belief that I could make it at the bar despite my lack of family or personal connections. (They also stood or sat through interminable debating competitions, rugby matches, swimming galas and plays as I was growing up!)

So many teachers were responsible for showing me how to challenge ideas and think for myself. Graham Finch and Jon

Knight devoted hundreds of unpaid hours to running the debating and mock trial programmes at school that gave me my first opportunity to get on my feet. Jane Stevens coached me from a shy ten-year-old to a (no doubt annoyingly) assertive young adult. Dr Stephen Tyre at the University of St Andrews patiently endured every weird historical theory I advanced as an undergraduate (not to mention my attempt to make mulled wine in his kettle), and endowed me with the forensic skills that I use every day in practice. Professor Rosa Freedman, despite being assigned to teach me land law, took me for coffee and pushed me to pursue constitutional law and human rights. Professors Eric Heinze and Merris Amos, my PhD supervisors, not only taught me to develop academic ideas but pushed me to read Austen and Hemingway so that I could find a way to express them in a manner that didn't give the reader a migraine (sincere apologies for all the times I have fallen below that standard in the preceding pages).

My pupil supervisors, Ryan Kholi, Estelle Dehon and Clare Parry, taught me everything I know about practice at the bar. My clerks (particularly Elliot Langdorf, Daniel Gatt, George/(Alex) Regan and Chelsea Thomas) supported me in developing my own practice, even when my ideas seemed a little off the wall. And the whole of Cornerstone Barristers took a chance in giving me pupillage and then tenancy. Aidan O'Neill QC, Elaine Motion and David Welsh gave me one of the greatest opportunities of my life when they let me (despite only having been in practice for less than a year) join their team for the most significant constitutional case in nearly half a century. Geraint Davies MP has brought me into parliamentary decision-making since I was a doctoral student.

I'm incredibly grateful to all of the solicitors and lay clients who have instructed me on so many interesting matters, particularly Erin Alcock and Rosa Curling at Leigh Day, Dr Christopher Stanley at KRW, Katie Wheatley and Hester Cavaciuti at Bindmans and Kate Harrison at Harrison Grant.

During the time I was writing this book I was technically homeless (having made the extremely foolish decision to sell our flat at the very start of the first coronavirus lockdown). My in-laws, Monica and Tony, took my wife and me in and housed (and fed!) us for over a year. My brother, Joe Fowles, provided a font of economic and public policy wisdom and didn't let me get away with any bad ideas, and Philip Kolvin QC read early drafts. My brother- and sister-in-law, Mark and Jen Grace, kept things light throughout lockdown (when I was freaking out about the challenges of writing a whole book on my own) with hours of beer pong and plates of increasingly hot buffalo wings.

My agent Sophie Lambert helped me develop this book from the very earliest proposals and worked unbelievably hard to get it published. Everyone at Oneworld has gone above and beyond for this project. Particularly my editor, Cecilia Stein, who pushed me to develop the project from the book that I thought people would want to read into the one I really wanted to write and who has devoted countless hours to making every part of it better.

Finally, and most importantly, my wife, Vicki Grace, who not only supports, challenges and inspires me every day but also raised the money to fund the Clapham/Bristol Inquiry.

Also, Archie the dog.

# NOTES

## Introduction

1 Wallis, N., *The Great Post Office Scandal* (London: Bath Publishing, 2021).

2 Sinclair, L., 'Post Office worker took his own life after being wrongly accused of stealing £60K', *Evening Standard* (24 April 2021), available at https://www.standard.co.uk/news/uk/post-office-scandal-worker-suicide-wrongly-accused-stealing-b931504.html (last accessed 4 January 2022 ).

3 Levitsky, S. and Ziblatt, D., *How Democracies Die: What History Reveals About Our Future* (New York: Penguin, 2018).

4 Platt, E. and Parker, G., 'UK credit rating downgraded by Moody's', *Financial Times* (16 October 2020), available at https://www.ft.com/content/117349e4-dc95-4509-969b-26dcdede1773 (last accessed 26 November 2020).

5 Abraham Lincoln, 'The Gettysburg Address' (19 November 1863), available at http://www.abrahamlincolnonline.org/lincoln/speeches/gettysburg.htm (last accessed 19 June 2020).

6 See Frankfurt, H., *On Bullshit* (New Jersey: Princeton University Press, 2005).

## Chapter 1: The Lodestar of the Constitution

1 'Lengths of prorogation since 1900', House of Lords Library (2019),

available at https://lordslibrary.parliament.uk/research-briefings/
lln-2019-0111/ (last accessed 2 October 2020).

2 It's worth noting that while 'breaking the deadlock' describes the
Supreme Court's task, in practice it isn't technically correct. Both the
decision of the High Court and the Court of Session were appealed.
The Supreme Court would, therefore, likely have been asked to rule
on prorogation even if the Scots and English courts agreed.

3 Gregory, A. and Smith, M., 'Tory Liam Fox doesn't regret saying the
Brexit talks would be the easiest negotiation in history', *Mirror* (22
October 2017), available at https://www.mirror.co.uk/news/poli-
tics/tory-liam-fox-doesnt-regret-11387919 (last accessed 2 October
2020).

4 'Daniel Hannan on Channel 4 News discussing Britain's EU referendum', YouTube, available at https://www.youtube.com/
watch?v=zzykce4oxII (last accessed 2 October 2020).

5 Finnis, J., 'Only one option remains with Brexit – prorogue Parliament
and allow us out of the EU with no-deal', *Telegraph* (1 April 2019),
available at https://www.telegraph.co.uk/politics/2019/04/01/one
-option-remains-brexit-prorogue-parliament-allow-us-eu/ (last accessed 2 October 2020).

6 Rourke, A., '"Mad suggestion": how Tory ministers once viewed the
call to prorogue parliament', *Guardian* (29 August 2019), available at
https://www.theguardian.com/politics/2019/aug/29/mad-sugges-
tion-how-tory-ministers-once-viewed-call-to-prorogue-parliament
(last accessed 2 October 2020).

7 Elaine Bradshaw, Chair of Balfour and Manson, was our solicitor; we
were advised by Professor Kenneth Armstrong of Cambridge Univ.

8 House of Lords Library, 'Lengths of prorogations since 1900' (2019),
available at https://lordslibrary.parliament.uk/research-briefings/
lln-2019-0111/ (last accessed 22 June 2021).

9 *R v Secretary of State for the Home Department, Ex p Fire Brigades
Union* [1995] 2 AC 513 at 552.

10 Kellner, P., *Democracy: 1000 Years in Pursuit of British Liberty*
(London: Mainstream Publishing, 2009).

11 Ibid.

12 Ibid.

13 It might be argued that some form of the 'rule of law' existed during
the medieval and early modern periods. Monarchs from Athelstan to

Henry II attempted to impose national 'laws'. These, however, flowed from the person of the monarch and could be revised or dispensed with at his pleasure. 'Law', therefore, did not 'rule'. The king ruled *through* law but not *by* law.

14  See Mandicott, J. R., *The Origins of the English Parliament 924–1327* (London: Oxford University Press, 2012); Graves, M. A. R., *The Tudor Parliaments 1485–1603* (London: Routledge, 1985).

15  Kellner, *Democracy.*

16  Ibid.

17  *The Case of the Proclamations* [1610] 12 Coke Reports 74; 77 E.R. 1352.

18  *Somerset v Stewart* [1772] 98 E.R. 499.

19  Kellner, *Democracy.*

20  Ibid.

21  Hostettler, J., *Thomas Erskine and Trial by Jury* (Hook: Waterside Press, 2010).

22  Reid, R., *The Peterloo Massacre* (London: Windmill, 1989).

23  Weaver, M., 'The Birmingham Bullring Riots of 1839: Variations on a Theme of Class Conflict', 78 *Social Science Quarterly* 1 (1997).

24  Howlette, C. J., 'Writing on the Body: Representation and Resistance in British Suffragette Accounts of Forcible Feeding', 23 *Genders* 3 (1996).

25  See Cobain, I., *The History Thieves* (London: Portobello Books, 2016).

26  *Ghaidan v. Godin Mendoza* [2004] UKHL 30 [2004] 2 AC 557 at 132.

27  *Jackson v. Attorney General* [2006] 1 AC 262 at 104–6.

28  *Miller/Cherry* [2020] A.C. 273 at 55.

29  Dicey, A. V., *The Law of the Constitution*, 10th ed. (London: Macmillan, 1956), pp. 434–5.

30  As Lord Browne-Wilkinson put it in *R v Secretary of State for the Home Department, Ex p Fire Brigades Union* [1995] 2 AC 513: '[T]he constitutional history of this country is the history of the prerogative powers of the Crown being made subject to the over-riding powers of the *democratically elected legislature* as the sovereign body.'

31  Mill, J. S., *Considerations on Representative Government* (Cambridge: Cambridge University Press, 2010; first published 1861).

32  [1968] AC 997; [1985] A.C. 374 ('GCHQ').
33  *Miller/Cherry* [2020] A.C. 273 at 41 and 46.

# Chapter 2: Lies, Damn Lies and Bullshit

1  Kellner, *Democracy*.

2  Cartledge, P., *Democracy: A Life* (London: Oxford University Press, 2016).

3  Clohesy, W. W., 'Democracy as Trust in Public Discourse' (2007), *Forum on Public Policy: A Journal of the Oxford Roundtable*, pp. 1–26.

4  Ipsos MORI, 'The Perils of Perception 2018' (6 December 2018), available at https://www.ipsos.com/ipsos-mori/en-uk/perils-perception-2018 (last accessed 18 September 2020).

5  Paige, J., 'British public wrong about nearly everything, survey shows', *Independent* (17 February 2014), available at https://www.independent.co.uk/news/uk/home-news/british-public-wrong-about-nearly-everything-survey-shows-8697821.html (last accessed 10 November 2020).

6  Frankfurt, H., 'On Bullshit', *Raritan*, 6 (2), 1986.

7  Frankfurt, 'On Bullshit'.

8  Dunt, I., 'What one piece of Jacob Rees-Mogg nonsense tells us about Brexit tactics', Politics.co.uk (21 May 2018), available at https://www.politics.co.uk/blogs/2018/05/21/what-one-piece-of-jacob-rees-mogg-nonsense-tells-us-about-br (last accessed 17 November 2020).

9  'Boris Johnson's letter to MPs in full', BBC (28 August 2019), available at https://www.bbc.co.uk/news/uk-politics-49497667 (last accessed 18 September 2020).

10  Zeffman, H., 'Ask the Queen to suspend Parliament, Rees-Mogg urges May', *The Times* (23 January 2019), available at https://www.thetimes.co.uk/article/ask-the-queen-to-suspend-parliament-rees-mogg-urges-may-l5fzgbkcf (last accessed 18 September 2020).

11  *Cherry v Lord Advocate* [2019] CSIH 49 at 53.

12  Oborne, P., *Assault on Truth: Boris Johnson, Donald Trump, and the Emergence of a New Moral Barbarism* (London: Simon and Schuster, 2021).

13  Hopkin, J. and Rosamond, B., 'Post-truth Politics, Bullshit, and Bad

Ideas: "Deficit Fetishism" in the UK', *New Political Economy*, 23 (6), 2018, pp. 641–5.

14 Standing, G., *The Corruption of Capitalism: Why rentiers thrive and work does not pay* (London: Biteback, 2016).

15 Proctor, K., Mason, R. and Stewart, H., 'Tories forced into a climb-down over claim aide was hit by Labour protestor', *Guardian* (9 December 2019), available at https://www.theguardian.com/politics/2019/dec/09/matt-hancock-aide-altercation-hospital-campaign-visit (last accessed 18 September 2020).

16 Merrick, R., 'Tory party urges activists to campaign like Trump by "weaponising fake news" and "fighting wokeism"', *Independent* (15 December 2020), available at https://www.independent.co.uk/news/uk/politics/tory-activists-trump-wellingborough-fake-news-b1774341.html (last accessed 23 July 2021).

17 Bienkov, A., Twitter (15 December 2020), available at https://twitter.com/adambienkov/status/1338790302769930247?s=21 (last accessed 23 July 2021).

18 Government Legal Department, Annual Report and Accounts 2020–21, available at https://assets.publishing.service.gov.uk/government/uploads/system/uploads/attachment_data/file/892679/Government_Legal_Department_Annual_Report_and_Accounts_2019-20.pdf (last accessed 10 November 2020). NOTE: The value quoted is the total value of goods and services purchased.

19 Farage, N., 'The will of the people deserves respect, not sneers, from Sir Alan Duncan and the liberal elite', *Telegraph* (3 July 2018), available at https://www.telegraph.co.uk/politics/2018/07/03/will-people-deserves-respect-not-sneers-sir-alan-duncan-liberal/ (last accessed 4 January 2022).

20 Curtis, L. P., *Anglo-Saxons and Celts: A Study of Anti-Irish Prejudice in Victorian England* (New York: Oxford University Press, 1968), p. 51.

21 Stocker, P., *English Uprising: Brexit and the Mainstreaming of the Far Right* (London: Melville House, 2017).

22 Norton-Taylor, R., 'The Zinoviev letter was a dirty trick by MI6', *Guardian* (4 February 1999), available at https://www.theguardian.com/politics/1999/feb/04/uk.politicalnews6 (last accessed 21 September 2020).

23 'The Times view of the prime minister's suitability for No 10: Johnson Adrift', *The Times* (18 September 2020), available at https://www.

thetimes.co.uk/article/the-times-view-on-the-prime-ministers-suit-ability-for-no-10-johnson-adrift-lxkxzcct3 (last accessed 18 September 2020).

24  *R (Miller) v Prime Minister* [2020] A.C. 373 at 1.

25  Doyle, J., Martin, A. and Doughty, S., 'Jacob Rees-Mogg accuses the Supreme Court of a "constitutional coup" over its stunning ruling', *Daily Mail* (24 September 2019), available at https://www.dailymail.co.uk/news/article-7500543/Jacob-Rees-Mogg-accuses-Supreme-Court-constitutional-coup-stunning-ruling.html (last accessed 21 September 2020).

26  Cecil, N., 'Attorney General Geoffrey Cox in Twitter spat with professor over Supreme Court verdict', *Evening Standard*, (25 September 2019) available at: https://www.standard.co.uk/news/politics/attorney-general-geoffrey-cox-in-twitter-spat-with-professor-over-the-supreme-court-verdict-a4246101.html (last accessed 14 March 2022).

27  The Conservative Party, 'Get Brexit Done: Unleash Britain's Potential' (2019), available at https://assets-global.website-files.com/5da42e2cae7ebd3f8bde353c/5dda924905da587992a064ba_Conservative%202019%20Manifesto.pdf (last accessed 21 September 2020).

28  O'Toole, F., *Heroic Failure: Brexit and the Politics of Pain* (London: Apollo, 2018).

29  Merrick, R., 'Government misrepresented my report to make assault on judicial review, says former Tory minister', *Independent* (16 June 2021), available at https://www.independent.co.uk/news/uk/politics/lord-faulks-tory-minister-judicial-review-b1867159.html (last accessed 21 July 2021).

30  https://www.gov.uk/government/groups/independent-review-of-administrative-law (last accessed 21 July 2021).

31  Hopewell, T., 'The Horrible History of the Daily Mail', Global Justice Now (31 October 2017), available at https://www.globaljustice.org.uk/blog/2017/oct/31/horrible-history-daily-mail (last accessed 18 November 2020); Doward, J., McVeigh, T., 'Royals told: open archives on family ties to Nazi regime', *Guardian* (18 July 2015), available at https://www.theguardian.com/uk-news/2015/jul/18/royal-family-archives-queen-nazi-salute (last accessed 18 November 2020).

32  Carr, E. H., *What Is History?* (London: Penguin, 1961).

33  Levitsky and Ziblatt, *How Democracies Die*.

34  Gove, M., 'Why does the left insist on belittling Britain's true heroes', *Daily Mail* (2 January 2014).

35  Kumar, K., 'Nation and empire: English and British national identity in comparative perspective', *Theory and Society*, 29 (5), 2000, pp. 575–608.

36  See, for example, Kumar, 'Nation and empire'.

37  Von Tunzelmann, A., 'The Imperial Myths Driving Brexit', *The Atlantic* (12 August 2019), available at https://www.theatlantic.com /international/archive/2019/08/imperial-myths-behind-brexit/ 595813/ (last accessed 18 November 2020).

38  Stone, J., 'Boris Johnson said colonialism in Africa should never have ended and dismissed Britain's role in slavery', *Independent* (13 June 2020); Wagner, K. A., 'Rees-Mogg's book is "sentimental jingoism and empire nostalgia"', *Guardian* (19 May 2019), available at https:/ /www.theguardian.com/books/2019/may/19/jacob-rees-mogg-victorians-sentimental-jingoism-and-empire-nostalgia (last accessed 18 November 2020).

39  McQuade, J., 'Colonialism was a disaster and the facts prove it', The Conversation (27 September 2017), available at https://theconver-sation.com/colonialism-was-a-disaster-and-the-facts-prove-it-84496 (last accessed 21 July 2021); see, for example, Tharoor, S., *Inglorious Empire: What the British Did to India* (London: Penguin, 2018).

40  Jenrick, R., 'We will save Britain's statues from the woke militants who want to censor our past', *Telegraph* (19 January 2021), available at https://www.telegraph.co.uk/news/2021/01/16/will-save-brit-ains-statues-woke-militants-want-censor-past/ (last accessed 27 March 2021).

41  Roberts, A. and Gebreyohanes, Z., 'Churchill College has made a wise decision in closing down the working group on Churchill, Race and Empire', Policy Exchange (18 June 2021), available at https:// policyexchange.org.uk/churchill-college-has-made-a-wise-decision-in-closing-down-the-working-group-on-churchill-race-and-empire/ (last accessed 21 July 2021).

42  See link at https://www.younghistoriansproject.org/single-post/ 2020/07/06/not-in-our-name (last accessed 21 July 2021).

43 Stubley, P., 'Museums risk funding cuts if they remove controversial objects, culture secretary warns', *Independent* (27 September 2020), available at https://www.independent.co.uk/news/uk/politics/statues-british-museum-government-funding-black-lives-matter-oliver-dowden-b651318.html (last accessed 18 November 2020); Trilling, D., 'Why is the UK government suddenly targeting "critical race theory"?', *Guardian* (23 October 2020), available at https://www.theguardian.com/commentisfree/2020/oct/23/uk-critical-race-theory-trump-conservatives-structural-inequality (last accessed 27 March 2021).

44 Matharu, H., 'Anti-woke crusade igniting threats to safety and careers', Byline Times (11 February 2021), available at https://bylinetimes.com/2021/02/11/anti-woke-crusade-igniting-threats-to-safety-and-careers-theres-so-much-hatred-projected-at-women-in-public-life-warns-historian/ (last accessed 27 March 2021).

45 Finnis, J., 'The unconstitutionality of the Supreme Court's prorogation judgment', *Policy Exchange* (2019), available at https://policy-exchange.org.uk/wp-content/uploads/2019/10/The-unconstitutionality-of-the-Supreme-Courts-prorogation-judgment.pdf (last accessed 22 July 2021).

46 Craig, P., 'Judicial Power, the Judicial Power Project and the UK', *Articles by Maurer Faculty*, 2670, 2017.

47 Powerbase, 'Policy Exchange', available at https://powerbase.info/index.php/Policy_Exchange (last accessed 25 November 2020).

48 Craig, 'Judicial Power, the Judicial Power Project and the UK'.

49 Judicial Power Project, available at: https://judicialpowerproject.org.uk/about/ (last accessed 14 March 2022).

50 Poole, T., 'The Executive Power Project', *London Review of Books* (2 April 2019).

# Chapter 3: Zombie Parliament

1 See, for example, Mullin, C., *A Very British Coup* (London: Serpent's Tail, 2010).

2 'Withdrawal Agreement: Commission sends letter of formal notice to the United Kingdom for breach of its obligations under

the Protocol on Ireland and Northern Ireland', European Commission (15 March 2021), available at https://ec.europa.eu/commission/presscorner/detail/en/ip_21_1132 (last accessed 14 July 2021).

3 'Northern Ireland Secretary admits new bill will "break international law"' (8 September 2020), available at https://www.bbc.co.uk/news/uk-politics-54073836 (last accessed 14 July 2021).

4 Curtice, J., 'Do voters support a no-deal Brexit?', BBC (4 September 2019), available at https://www.bbc.co.uk/news/uk-politics-49551893 (last accessed 14 July 2021).

5 Runciman, D., *How Democracy Ends* (London: Profile Books, 2019).

6 Prince, R., *Standing Down: Interviews with Retiring MPs* (London: Biteback Publishing, 2015).

7 There are some opportunities for MPs to determine their own business. Twenty days are set aside for 'opposition business'. Ministerial and prime ministerial questions, early day motions and Westminster Hall debates are all determined by MPs. These, however, are all 'non-binding' in effect. A minister may have a hard time during questions or debate, but s/he is not required to do anything as a result. A bad showing may have a political effect but most of the time this is relatively minor. Prime Minister's Questions, the most watched proceeding in parliament, ranks outside the top 200 most popular TV programmes in the UK. To give this some context, it is beaten out by, among others, *Judge Rinder* and *Grand Canal Journeys*. See, YouGov, 'The most popular contemporary TV programmes in the UK', available at https://yougov.co.uk/ratings/media/popularity/current-tv-programmes/all (last accessed 12 November 2020). MPs are allowed to argue against the government, but only for show. When it comes to the crunch, the executive remains firmly in control.

8 Hardman, I., *Why We Get the Wrong Politicians* (London: Atlantic, 2018).

9 *Hansard* HC Deb. vol. 691 cols. 198ff. (16 March 2021).

10 'Keir Starmer – 2020 Speech on the Future Relationship with the EU Bill', UKPol.co.uk (30 December 2020), available at https://www.ukpol.co.uk/keir-starmer-2020-speech-on-the-future-relationship-with-the-eu-bill/ (last accessed 4 January 2022).

11 Cooper, L. and Fowles, S., 'Parliament should have a meaningful vote on the EU trade deal. But it doesn't', Foreign Policy Centre (30

December 2020), available at https://fpc.org.uk/parliament-should -have-a-meaningful-vote-on-the-eu-trade-deal-but-it-doesnt/ (last accessed 14 July 2021).

12 Waterson, J., 'Vote Leave strategist refuses to appear before MPs in fake news inquiry', *Guardian* (17 May 2018), available at https:// www.theguardian.com/politics/2018/may/17/vote-leave-strategist -dominic-cummings-refuses-to-appear-before-mps (last accessed 17 August 2020).

13 Syal, R., 'Dominic Cummings found in contempt of parliament', *Guardian* (27 March 2019), available at https://www.theguardian. com/politics/2019/mar/27/commons-report-rules-dominic-cummings-in-contempt-of-parliament (last accessed 17 August 2020).

14 Woodcock, A., 'Government accused of undermining scrutiny of EU trade deal, as Jacob Rees-Mogg shuts down Commons Brexit committee', *Independent* (8 January 2021), available at https:// www.independent.co.uk/news/uk/politics/brexit-committee-jacob-rees-mogg-eu-trade-deal-b1784512.html (last accessed 4 January 2022).

15 'Johnson defends language after criticism from MPs', BBC (26 September 2019), available at https://www.bbc.co.uk/news/uk-politics-49843363 (last accessed 12 November 2020).

16 Walpole, J. and Kelly, R., 'The Whip's Office', House of Commons Library (10 October 2008).

17 Levitsky and Ziblatt, *How Democracies Die*.

18 Hardman, *Why We Get the Wrong Politicians*.

19 Ibid.

20 'Boris Johnson: "I'd rather be dead in a ditch" than ask for Brexit delay', BBC (5 September 2019), available at https://www.bbc.co.uk /news/av/uk-politics-49601128/boris-johnson-i-d-rather-be-dead-in-a-ditch-than-ask-for-brexit-delay (last accessed 4 January 2022).

21 'Prime Minister's statement: 2 September 2019', available at https:// www.gov.uk/government/speeches/prime-ministers-statement-2-september-2019; *Hansard* HC Deb. vol. 664 col. 140 (3 September 2019), available at http://bit.ly/2zSD79W; 'Boris Johnson rules out asking Brussels for a delay to Brexit', *Financial Times* (3 September 2019), available at https://www.ft.com/video/762875f8-810b-41b3-8b8d-517b71e85f10?playlist-name=less-than-90

-seconds&playlist-offset=0; *Hansard* HC Deb. vol. 664 cols 26–7 (3 September 2019), available at http://bit.ly/2LxZdnT; Stefanovic, P., Twitter (3 September 2019), available at https://twitter.com/PeterStefanovi2/status/1168800398976716800; *Hansard* HC Deb. vol. 664 cols 27–8 (3 September 2019), available at http://bit.ly/2NUJxxT; *Hansard* HC Deb. vol. 664 cols 291–2 (4 September 2019), available at http://bit.ly/2NWDHvX; *Hansard* HC Deb. vol. 664 col. 164 (4 September 2019), available at https://t.co/mZGpwXvw5u?amp=1; 'Boris Johnson: "I'd rather be dead in a ditch" than ask for Brexit delay', BBC (5 September 2019), available at https://www.bbc.co.uk/news/av/uk-politics-49601128/boris-johnson-i-d-rather-be-dead-in-a-ditch-than-ask-for-brexit-delay; https://us.v-cdn.net/5020679/uploads/editor/bt/yqmxleaak73q.jpg; *Telegraph*, Twitter (6 September 2019), available at https://twitter.com/Telegraph/status/1170085737154469890/photo/1; 'Government will "test to the limit" law designed to stop no-deal Brexit', ITV (8 September 2019), available at https://www.itv.com/news/2019-09-08/tory-party-fractures-as-boris-johnson-digs-in-over-brexit-delay/; Shipman, T., and Wheeler, C., 'Boris Johnson "to break law for Brexit" as he snatches 14-point lead over Corbyn', *The Times* (8 September 2019), available at https://www.thetimes.co.uk/article/04c0a540-d1ac-11e9-b36a-8cbd36fa980c; Bennett, O., and Yorke, H., 'Boris Johnson draws up plan to legally stop Brexit extension if MPs vote against general election', *Telegraph* (8 September 2019), available at https://www.telegraph.co.uk/politics/2019/09/08/boris-johnson-draws-plan-legally-stop-brexit-extension-mps-vote/; Sparrow, A., et al., 'Chaotic scenes in the Commons as parliament is suspended – as it happened', *Guardian* (10 September 2019), available at https://www.theguardian.com/politics/live/2019/sep/09/brexit-latest-news-eu-no-deal-bill-royal-assent-boris-johnson-parliament-politics-live; *Hansard* HC Deb. vol. 664 col. 619 (9 September 2019), available at https://hansard.parliament.uk/commons/2019-09-09/debates/44BDF5ED-3C22-40B5-AAD8-1EA95DED732C/EarlyParliamentaryGeneralElection(No2); Peston, R., Twitter (10 September 2019), available at https://twitter.com/Peston/status/1171532751024996352?s=19; *The Andrew Marr Show* (8 September 2019), transcript available at http://news.bbc.co.uk/1/shared/bsp/hi/pdfs/08091902.pdf; Rozenberg, J.,

Twitter (8 September 2019), available at https://twitter.com/ JoshuaRozenberg/status/1170589084882034688; Coates, S., Twitter (15 September 2019), available at https://twitter.com/ samcoatessky/status/1173140164081868800?s=21; 'Dominic Cummings says news "almost all bull\*\*\*" when asked about Brexit language row', Sky (27 September 2019), available at https://news. sky.com/video/cummings-calls-news-as-almost-all-bull-when-pressed-about-his-masterplan-11820481, see 00:25; Helm, T., 'Johnson to tell Juncker: "I won't discuss Brexit extension beyond 31 October', *Guardian* (15 September 2019), available at https://www. theguardian.com/politics/2019/sep/15/johnson-to-defy-benn-bill -quit-31-october-come-what-may; 'In full: Boris Johnson interview from Luxembourg with BBC's Laura Kuenssberg', BBC (16 September 2019), available at https://www.bbc.co.uk/news/uk-politics-49717554; Peston, R., Twitter (25 September 2019), available at https://twitter.com/Peston/status/1176829346826338304; *Hansard* HC Deb. vol. 664 cols 774–5 (25 September 2019), available at https://hansard.parliament.uk/Commons/2019-09-25/ debates/AD2A07E5-9741-4EBA-997A-97776F80AA38/ PrimeMinisterSUpdate; https://www.bbc.co.uk/sounds/play/ p07pgq94 at 14:05; *Hansard* HC Deb. vol. 664 col. 851 (26 September 2019), available at https://hansard.parliament.uk/ commons/2019-09-26/debates/4BFC992D-7B89-467B-9042-0B8345943D39/ComplianceWithTheEuropeanUnion(With-drawal)(No2)Act 2019; *The Andrew Marr Show* (29 Sept. 2019), available at https://www.bbc.co.uk/iplayer/episode/m0008zpf/the -andrew-marr-show-29092019; Proctor, K., 'Boris Johnson fuels speculation he could ignore Brexit delay law', *Guardian* (29 September 2019), available at https://www.theguardian.com/poli-tics/2019/sep/29/boris-johnson-fuels-speculation-could-ignore-brexit-delay-law; 'Tory conference: National Living Wage to rise to £10.50, says chancellor', BBC (30 September 2019), available at https://www.bbc.co.uk/news/uk-politics-49881980; Elliott, F., and Swinford, S., 'Block Brexit delay, Boris Johnson urges EU', *The Times* (1 October 2019), available at https://www.thetimes.co.uk/edition/ news/block-brexit-delay-boris-johnson-urges-eu-d3wrqhvwb; Balls, K., 'The Tories can live with a Brexit extension – as long as someone else takes the blame', *Guardian* (30 September 2019), available at

https://www.theguardian.com/commentisfree/2019/sep/30/
tories-brexit-extension-31-october.

22 *Dale Vince and Ors v The Prime Minister and Advocate General* [2019]
CSOH 77.

23 Boffey, D., 'Brexit: Johnson sends unsigned letter asking for delay,
and second arguing against it', *Guardian* (20 October 2019), available at https://www.theguardian.com/politics/2019/oct/19/eu-will
-grant-brexit-extension-if-johnson-sends-letter-says-brussels    (last
accessed 4 January 2022).

24 'Brexit: European Council adopts decision to extend the period
under Article 50' (29 October 2019), available at https://www.
consilium.europa.eu/en/press/press-releases/2019/10/29/brexit-
european-council-adopts-decision-to-extend-the-period-under-arti-
cle-50/ (last accessed 4 January 2022).

25 'Speaker criticised for "flagrant abuse" of parliamentary process', ITV
(8 September 2019), available at https://www.itv.com/news/2019-
09-08/speaker-criticised-for-allowing-flagrant-abuse-of-parliamen-
tary-process (last accessed 18 August 2020).

26 PA Media, 'Tories plan to contest John Bercow's seat in breach of
convention', *Guardian* (8 September 2019), available at https://
www.theguardian.com/politics/2019/sep/08/tories-contest-
speaker-john-bercow-seat-breach-convention-andrea-leadsom-
brexit (last accessed 18 August 2020).

27 Elgot J., "Rude and threatening': the main findings of the John
Bercow bullying inquiry', *Guardian*, (8 March 2022), available at:
https://www.theguardian.com/politics/2022/mar/08/rude-and-
threatening-the-main-findings-of-the-john-bercow-bullying-inquiry
(last accessed 14 March 2022).

28 *Hansard* HC Deb. vol. 675 col. 2 (21 April 2020) and HC Deb. vol.
674 col. 74 (22 April 2020).

29 Murphy, J., 'PMQs preview: Sir Keir Starmer will rise, and MPs will
hold their breath in anticipation', *Evening Standard* (19 May 2020),
available at https://www.standard.co.uk/news/politics/pmqs-sir-
keir-starmer-boris-johnson-preview-a4445326.html (last accessed
18 August 2020).

30 Hyde, M., 'Without his frontbench cheerleaders, Johnson has
nowhere to hide', *Guardian* (15 May 2020), available at https://
www.theguardian.com/commentisfree/2020/may/15/boris

-johnson-keir-starmer-frontbench-cheerleaders (last accessed 18 August 2020).

31 *Hansard* HC Deb. vol. 676 col. 602 (20 May 2020).

32 *Hansard* HC Deb. vol. 676 col. 275 (2 June 2020).

33 Duffield, C., 'Ending hybrid Parliament could leave MPs with health conditions shut out of votes, politicians fear', *i* (30 May 2020), available at https://inews.co.uk/news/ending-hybrid-parliament-could-leave-mps-health-conditions-shut-out-votes-432574 (last accessed 18 August 2020).

34 Gordon, R., 'Why Henry VIII Clauses Should be Consigned to the Dustbin of History', Public Law Project, available at https://publiclawproject.org.uk/content/uploads/data/resources/220/WHY-HENRY-VIII-CLAUSES-SHOULD-BE-CONSIGNED-TO-THE-DUSTBIN-OF-HISTORY.pdf (last accessed 11 November 2020); in 1932 the Donoughmore Committee (Gaus, J. M., 'The Report of the British Committee on Ministers' Powers', *American Political Science Review*, 26 (6), 1932, pp. 1142–7), tasked with reviewing the government and parliament's use of delegated legislation, concluded that Henry VIII clauses should be strongly discouraged. If such a clause was to be used, the committee concluded, then it must be 'demonstrably essential' and ministers had a duty to justify it 'to the hilt'.

35 Allen, C. K., *Law and Orders. An Enquiry into the nature and scope of Delegated Legislation and Executive Powers in England* (London: Stevens and Sons, 1945), p. 102.

36 Gordon, 'Why Henry VIII Clauses Should be Consigned to the Dustbin of History'.

37 Select Committee on the Constitution, 'The Legislative Process: The Delegation of Powers', 2017–19, HL paper 225: the House of Lords Constitution Committee describes skeleton bills as lying at the 'extreme end of the spectrum of legislative uncertainty'. To a certain extent, of course, any Act that delegates powers to ministers is allowing the executive to make law. Until recently, however, the usual practice was to clearly define the policy area in which ministers were empowered to make secondary legislation and set out the things that they must take into account when doing so. Skeleton bills simply allow ministers to make whatever law they want.

38 Delegated Powers and Regulatory Reform Committee, 'Agriculture Bill', 2017–19, HL paper 194: the Lords Committee on Delegated

Powers and Regulatory Reform concluded: 'The Agriculture Bill represents a major transfer of powers from the EU to Ministers of the Crown, bypassing Parliament and the devolved legislatures in Wales and Northern Ireland. Parliament will not be able to debate the merits of the new agriculture regime because the Bill does not contain even an outline of the substantive law that will replace the CAP after the United Kingdom leaves the EU. Most debate will centre on delegated powers because most of the Bill is about delegated powers. At this stage it cannot even be said that the devil is in the detail, because the Bill contains so little detail.'

39  Select Committee on the Constitution, 'The Legislative Process', HL paper 225.

40  See https://www.ordnancesurvey.co.uk/election-maps/gb/.

41  Elliott, F., 'Redrawn constituency map will give Tories a ten-seat advantage', *The Times* (4 December 2020), available at https://www.thetimes.co.uk/article/redrawn-constituency-map-will-give-tories-a-ten-seat-advantage-m7xzjqfp2 (last accessed 20 March 2021).

42  '2019 electoral fraud data', The Electoral Commission, available at https://www.electoralcommission.org.uk/who-we-are-and-what-we-do/our-views-and-research/our-research/electoral-fraud-data/2019-electoral-fraud-data (last accessed 14 July 2021).

43  Palese, M., 'The government's own research shows millions of people may lack appropriate voter ID', Electoral Reform Society (14 May 2021), available at https://www.electoral-reform.org.uk/the-governments-own-research-shows-millions-of-people-may-lack-appropriate-voter-id/ (last accessed 14 July 2021).

44  Barton, C., 'GE2019: How did demographics affect the result?', House of Commons Library (21 February 2020), available at https://commonslibrary.parliament.uk/ge2019-how-did-demographics-affect-the-result/ (last accessed 14 July 2021).

45  Levine, S., 'Federal judge blocks North Carolina's voter ID law, citing its discriminatory intent', *Guardian* (1 January 2020), available at https://www.theguardian.com/us-news/2020/jan/01/north-carolina-voter-id-law-blocked-discriminatory (last accessed 20 March 2021).

46  Fowles, S., 'Boris Johnson is turning back the constitutional clock by scrapping Fixed Term Act', *The New European* (11 December 2020), available at https://www.theneweuropean.co.uk/brexit-news/

westminster-news/sam-fowles-on-fixed-term-parliament-act-6731308 (14 July 2021).

# Chapter 4: Justice Denied

1 *R (Wilson) v Prime Minister* [2019] EWCA Civ 304.
2 Lord Dyson, 'Is Judicial Review a Threat to Democracy?', Sultan Azlan Shah Lecture (November 2015).
3 UK Public Spending 2021, available at https://www.ukpublicspending.co.uk/government_expenditure.html (last accessed 12 October 2020); 'Budget 2020', HM Treasury, available at https://www.gov.uk/government/publications/budget-2020-documents/budget-2020 (last accessed 12 October 2020).
4 Lord Acton, 'Letter to Bishop Creighton dated 5 April 1887', in Figgis, J. N., and Laurence, R. V., (eds), *Historical Essays and Studies* (London: Macmillan, 1907).
5 *Pengarah Tanah dan Galian v Sri Lempah Enterprise* [1979] IMLJ 135.
6 Torrence, M., 'Maxwell-Fyfe and the Origins of the ECHR', J. Law Soc. Sc. (19 September 2011).
7 Hardman, *Why We Get The Wrong Politicians.*
8 Loft, P. and Apostolova, V., 'Acts and Statutory Instruments: the volume of UK legislation from 1950 to 2016', House of Commons Library (21 April 2017), available at https://commonslibrary.parliament.uk/research-briefings/cbp-7438/ (last accessed 26 September 2020). The data in this research shows a drop in secondary legislation from 2016 to 2019 (the 'May government years') which can be explained by parliament and the government's focus on Brexit, which led to parliamentary and executive time being spent increasingly on non-legislative activity.
9 *O'Reilly v Mackman* [1983] 2 A.C. 237.
10 Civil Justice Statistics 2000–2019, available at https://assets.publishing.service.gov.uk/government/uploads/system/uploads/attachment_data/file/806900/civil-Justice-stats-main-tables-Jan-Mar_2019.xlsx (last accessed 26 September 2020).
11 Spurrier, M. and Hickman, J., 'Public Bill Committee Briefing Paper Following Oral Evidence: Part 4 Criminal Justice And Courts Bill' (London: Public Law Project, 2014), available at https://

publiclawproject.org.uk/content/uploads/data/resources/171/PLP-The-number-of-JR-cases.pdf (last accessed 26 September 2020).

12 The exception to this is immigration claims. The rapidly increasing complexity of immigration law since the mid-1990s saw a corresponding increase in claims for judicial review. These are now dealt with almost entirely by the Upper Tribunal rather than the Administrative Court. In any case, since a peak in the early years of the last decade, the number of immigration and asylum claims have also declined. Given the labyrinthine complexity of much of immigration legislation, it would hardly be surprising if claims increased.

13 See, The Independent Review of Administrative Law (March 2021), available at: https://assets.publishing.service.gov.uk/government/uploads/system/uploads/attachment_data/file/970797/IRAL-report.pdf and The Independent Human Rights Act Review (December 2021) available at: https://assets.publishing.service.gov.uk/government/uploads/system/uploads/attachment_data/file/1040525/ihrar-final-report.pdf (last accessed 23 March 2022).

14 'The judge over your shoulder – a guide to good decision making', Government Legal Department, (5th edn, 2018), p. 31.

15 Levitsky and Ziblatt, *How Democracies Die*.

16 Rozenberg, J., 'Judges were right to snub Blunkett's dinner date', *Telegraph* (19 October 2006), available at https://www.telegraph.co.uk/news/uknews/1531796/Judges-were-right-to-snub-Blunketts-dinner-date.html (last accessed 13 October 2020).

17 Mellor, J., 'Patel's "rotten to the core" Home Office argues with Secret Barrister and it doesn't go well', The London Economic (10 October 2020), available at https://www.thelondoneconomic.com/news/patels-rotten-to-the-core-home-office-argues-with-secret-barrister-and-it-doesnt-go-well-204923/ (last accessed 13 October 2020).

18 Barrister, T. S., *Fake Law: The truth about justice in an age of lies* (London: Picador, 2020).

19 'Timeline: Blunkett Resignation', BBC (21 December 2004), available at http://news.bbc.co.uk/1/hi/uk_politics/4057715.stm (last accessed 13 October 2020).

20 Stadlen, N., 'Brief Encounter: David Blunkett', *Guardian* (9 October 2006).

21 Select Committee on Constitution, HL Sixth Report 2006–7,

§§45–46, available at https://publications.parliament.uk/pa/ld200607/ldselect/ldconst/151/15104.htm#a12 (last accessed 13 October 2020).

22 Wagner, A., 'Catgate: another myth used to trash human rights', *Guardian* (4 October 2011), available at https://www.theguardian.com/law/2011/oct/04/theresa-may-wrong-cat-deportation (last accessed 18 June 2020).

23 *Hansard* HC Deb. vol. 569 col. 163 (22 October 2013).

24 Gillett, F., 'Theresa May attacks "left-wing human rights lawyers harassing UK troops"', *Evening Standard* (5 October 2016), available at https://www.standard.co.uk/news/uk/theresa-may-attacks-leftwing-human-rights-lawyers-harassing-uk-troops-a3361716.html (last accessed 14 July 2021).

25 *Case of the Proclamations* 12 CO Rep 74, 77 E.R. 1352.

26 Dominic Raab MP quoted in Slack, J., 'Enemies of the people: Fury over "out of touch" judges who have "declared war on democracy" by defying 17.4m Brexit voters and who could trigger constitutional crisis', *Daily Mail* (3 November 2016).

27 Hussain, A., 'Legal Twitterati outrage over Home Office's "activist lawyer" tweet', Legal Cheek (27 August 2020), available at https://www.legalcheek.com/2020/08/legal-twitterati-outrage-over-home-offices-activist-lawyer-tweet/ (last accessed 13 November 2020).

28 Butler, M., Twitter (4 September 2020), available at https://twitter.com/MirandaButler3/status/1301793026461888512?s=20 (last accessed 13 November 2020).

29 Priti Patel, 'Speech to the Conservative Party Conference' (4 October 2020), available at https://www.youtube.com/watch?v=uFcDzRvWkAo&feature=emb_logo (last accessed 13 November 2020).

30 Bowcott, O., 'Criminal cases delayed across England as courts lie idle', *Guardian* (19 August 2019), available at https://www.theguardian.com/law/2019/aug/19/criminal-cases-delayed-across-england-and-wales-as-courts-lie-idle (last accessed 13 November 2020); Boris Johnson, 'Speech to the Conservative Party Conference' (6 October 2020), available at https://www.youtube.com/watch?v=Uymn-jVINLg&feature=emb_logo (last accessed 13 November 2020).

31 Slack, 'Enemies of the people'; Dominiczak, P., Hope, C., and McCann, K., 'Judges vs the people: Government ministers resigned

to losing appeal against High Court ruling', *Telegraph* (3 November 2016); editorial, 'After judges' Brexit block now your country really needs you: We MUST get out of the EU', *Daily Express* (4 November 2016).

32  Letts, Q., 'Judges blew their hallowed status with the Supreme Court ruling and will now be fair game for public scrutiny', *Sun* (24 September 2019), available at https://www.thesun.co.uk/news/9998887/judges-supreme-court-public-scrutiny/amp/ (last accessed 13 October 2020).

33  Barrister, *Fake Law*.

34  Barrister, *Fake Law*; Townsend, M., 'Lawyers claim knife attack at law firm was inspired by Priti Patel's rhetoric', *Guardian* (10 October 2020).

35  'Judicial Attitudes Survey', Judiciary (25 February 2021), available at https://www.judiciary.uk/announcements/judicial-attitudes-survey/ (last accessed 14 July 2021).

36  Wagner, A., 'A war on judicial review?', UK Human Rights Blog (19 November 2012), available at https://ukhumanrightsblog.com/2012/11/19/a-war-on-judicial-review/ (last accessed 13 November 2020).

37  Bowcott, 'Criminal cases delayed across England as courts lie idle'.

38  Marlow, J., 'The government sets out its proposals for judicial review reform', Hogan Lovells (19 December 2020), available at https://www.hoganlovells.com/en/blogs/focus-on-regulation/the-government-sets-out-its-proposals-for-judicial-review-reform (last accessed 13 November 2020).

39  Ekins, R., Morgan, J. and Tugendhat, T., 'Clearing the Fog of Law: Saving our armed forces from defeat by judicial diktat', Policy Exchange (2015), available at https://policyexchange.org.uk/wp-content/uploads/2016/09/clearing-the-fog-of-law.pdfhttps://policyexchange.org.uk/wp-content/uploads/2016/09/clearing-the-fog-of-law.pdf (last accessed 4 January 2022).

40  *Hansard* HC Deb vol. 683 cols 154–5 (3 November 2020).

41  Fowles, S., 'The Overseas Operations (Service personnel and Veterans) Bill 2019–2021: Briefing', Institute for Constitutional and Democratic Research (2020).

42  Representation of the People Act 1982, ss. 82 and 159.

43  Fowles, S., 'Briefing: The Internal Market Bill 2019–2021',

Institute for Constitutional and Democratic Research (2020); Fowles, S., 'Briefing: The Covert Human Intelligence Sources Bill 2019–2021', Institute for Constitutional and Democratic Research (2020).

44  https://bills.parliament.uk/bills/3035

45  Hickman, T., *Judicial Review*, (9 February 2017), available at: https://ukconstitutionallaw.org/2017/02/09/tom-hickman-public-laws-disgrace/ (last accessed 23 March 2022).

46  I'd prepared an application to limit my clients' liability to just £5,000 but, even if it had succeeded, this sum, when combined with the court fee, would have been unaffordable (it's approximately a third of what a minimum wage worker can expect to make in a year).

47  Bowcott, O., 'Legal aid: how has it changed in 70 years?', *Guardian* (26 December 2018), available at https://www.theguardian.com/law/2018/dec/26/legal-aid-how-has-it-changed-in-70-years (last accessed 17 June 2020).

48  Connelly, T., 'Revealed: 2,089 wannabe barristers submit 14,516 applications for just 224 pupillage spots', Legal Cheek (12 February 2018), available at https://www.legalcheek.com/2018/02/revealed-2089-wannabe-barristers-submit-14516-applications-for-just-224-pupillage-spots/ (last accessed 17 June 2020).

49  For example, Slack, J. and Doyle, J., 'Legal aid payouts to fat cat lawyers will be slashed by a third, says Justice Secretary', *Daily Mail* (10 April 2013), available at https://www.dailymail.co.uk/news/article-2306630/Legal-aid-payouts-fat-cat-lawyers-slashed-says-Justice-Secretary.html (last accessed 17 June 2020).

50  Ellison, C., 'Criminal Barrister: "I earn less than minimum wage"' BBC News, (7 January 2021) available at: https://www.bbc.co.uk/news/av/uk-55548821 (last accessed 23 February 2022).

51  Bowcott, O., Hill, A. and Duncan, P., 'Revealed: legal aid cuts forcing parents to give up fight for children', *Guardian* (26 December 2018), available at https://www.theguardian.com/law/2018/dec/26/revealed-legal-aid-cuts-forcing-parents-to-give-up-fight-for-children (last accessed 17 June 2020).

52  Ibid.

53  Langdon-Down, G., 'Death by a thousand cuts?', Law Gazette (11 November 2019), available at https://www.lawgazette.co.uk/

features/death-by-a-thousand-cuts/5102102.article (last accessed 17 June 2020).

54 'Access Denied? LASPO four years on: a Law Society Review', The Law Society (June 2017), available at https://www.lawsociety.org.uk/en/topics/research/laspo-4-years-on (last accessed 17 June 2020).

# Chapter 5: Too Much Government

1 Mason, R., 'Theresa May accuses Russia of interfering in elections and fake news', *Guardian* (14 November 2017), available at https://www.theguardian.com/politics/2017/nov/13/theresa-may-accuses-russia-of-interfering-in-elections-and-fake-news (last accessed 5 November 2020).

2 Ibid.

3 Sengupta, K., '"We have no objections": Security officials say secret Russia report being blocked by Boris Johnson can be published immediately', *Independent* (5 November 2019), available at https://www.independent.co.uk/news/uk/politics/russia-conservative-party-brexit-intelligence-uk-report-national-security-money-a9185116.html (last accessed 5 November 2020).

4 Ibid.

5 *Hansard* HC Deb. vol. 667 col. 647 (5 November 2019), available at https://hansard.parliament.uk/commons/2019-11-05/debates/AABC4DE9-4D70-4937-9AF5-D58CE7B0601D/IntelligenceAndSecurityCommitteeReportOnRussia (last accessed 5 November 2020); *Hansard* HL Deb. vol. 800 col. 1162 (5 November 2019), available at https://hansard.parliament.uk/lords/2019-11-05/debates/07B59333-D026-43D9-BCED-6C43C4D36520/IntelligenceAndSecurityCommitteeReport (last accessed 5 November 2020).

6 *Hansard* HC Deb. vol. 667 col. 647 (5 November 2019), available at https://hansard.parliament.uk/commons/2019-11-05/debates/AABC4DE9-4D70-4937-9AF5-D58CE7B0601D/IntelligenceAndSecurityCommitteeReportOnRussia (last accessed 5 November 2020).

7 *Kennedy v Charity Commission* [2014] UKSC 20.

8  *Hansard* HC Deb. vol. 650 cols 556–7 (3 December 2018).

9  Levitsky and Ziblatt, *How Democracies Die*.

10  Ibid.

11  Quoted in Marshall, G., *Constitutional Conventions: The Rules and Forms of Political Accountability* (Oxford: Oxford University Press, 1987), p. 61. In practice it rarely works like this. There are relatively few examples of ministers offering their resignations as a result of policy failures. Until relatively recently, however, ministers were likely to resign where they have been personally involved in an error. Those most often cited in support by proponents of the doctrine are Sir Thomas Dugdale, who resigned over the Crichel Down case in 1954, and Lord Carrington, who resigned over his failure to properly anticipate the defence needs of the Falkland Islands in 1982. The only example this century is Amber Rudd, who resigned in 2017 as a result of the Windrush scandal.

12  Marshall, *Constitutional Conventions*, p. 63.

13  Allen, N. and Bingham, J., 'The scandals that brought Peter Mandelson down twice before', *Telegraph* (3 October 2008), available at https://www.telegraph.co.uk/news/politics/labour/3130348/The-scandals-that-brought-Peter-Mandelson-down-twice-before.html (last accessed 22 August 2020).

14  'Treasury Minister David Laws resigns over expenses', BBC (29 May 2010), available at https://www.bbc.co.uk/news/10191524 (last accessed 22 August 2020); Partridge, J., 'UK nominates Liam Fox to lead World Trade Organization', *Guardian* (8 July 2020), available at https://www.theguardian.com/world/2020/jul/08/uk-nominates-liam-fox-world-trade-organization (last accessed 24 August 2020); Syal, R. and Asthana A., 'Priti Patel forced to resign over unofficial meetings with Israelis', *Guardian* (8 November 2017), available at https://www.theguardian.com/politics/2017/nov/08/priti-patel-forced-to-resign-over-unofficial-meetings-with-israelis (last accessed 24 August 2020); Stewart, H., Gentleman, A. and Hopkins, N., 'Amber Rudd resigns hours after Guardian publishes deportation targets letter', *Guardian* (30 April 2018), available at https://www.theguardian.com/politics/2018/apr/29/amber-rudd-resigns-as-home-secretary-after-windrush-scandal (last accessed 24 August 2020); Stewart, H., Sabbagh, D. and Walker, P., 'Gavin Williamson: "I was tried by kangaroo court

– then sacked"', *Guardian* (1 May 2019), available at https://www. theguardian.com/politics/2019/may/01/gavin-williamson-sacked-as-defence-secretary-over-huawei-leak (last accessed 24 August 2020).

15 Savage, M. and Ford, R., 'Tory minister Dominic Grieve "was sacked after taking stand on ECHR"', *The Times* (21 July 2014), available at https://www.thetimes.co.uk/article/tory-minister-dominic-grieve-was-sacked-after-taking-stand-on-echr-skhh9kg5jjp (last accessed 24 August 2020).

16 Proctor, K., 'Adviser sacked by Cummings may have case for unfair dismissal – expert', *Guardian* (1 September 2019), available at https://www.theguardian.com/politics/2019/sep/01/adviser-sacked-by-cummings-may-have-case-for-unfair-dismissal-expert (last accessed 15 July 2021).

17 Durrant, T., Blacklaws, N. and Zodgekar, K., 'Special advisers and the Johnson government', Institute for Government (2020), available at https://www.instituteforgovernment.org.uk/sites/default/files/publications/special-advisers-johnson-government.pdf (last accessed 15 July 2021).

18 Elgot, J., 'Radical shake-up of civil service comms to be in place by April 2022', *Guardian* (16 March 2021), available at https://www.theguardian.com/politics/2021/mar/16/radical-shake-up-of-civil-service-comms-to-be-in-place-by-april-2022 (last accessed 15 July 2021).

19 Grossman, R., 'GCS 2020 – Making the Best, Standard' (16 October 2019), available at https://gcs.civilservice.gov.uk/blog/gcs-2020-making-the-best-standard/ (last accessed 15 July 2021).

20 Holder, S., 'A century of government communications', Civil Service Quarterly (2 July 2018), available at https://quarterly.blog.gov.uk/2018/07/02/a-century-of-government-communications/ (last accessed 24 August 2020).

21 Riddell, P., Letter to Lord Evans KCB DL (7 October 2020).

22 Pemberton, A., 'TalkTalk boss Dido Harding's utter ignorance is a lesson to us all', *Campaign* (27 October 2015), available at https://www.campaignlive.co.uk/article/talk-talk-boss-dido-hardings-utter-ignorance-lesson-us/1370062?src_site=marketingmagazine (last accessed 6 November 2020).

23 Volpicelli, G. M., 'How Test and Trace failed', *Wired* (5 November

2020), available at https://www.wired.co.uk/article/nhs-test-and-trace-covid-19-failure (last accessed 6 November 2020).

24 Cobain, *The History Thieves*.

25 Syal, R., 'Freedom of information commission not very free with its information', *Guardian* (9 October 2015), available at https://www.theguardian.com/politics/2015/oct/09/freedom-of-information-commission-not-very-free-with-its-information (last accessed 6 November 2020).

26 Craig, 'Judicial Power, the Judicial Power Project and the UK'.

27 Ministry of Housing, Communities and Local Government, 'Planning for the future' (2020). This paper was not given the reference usually used for white papers. It is available online at https://www.gov.uk/government/consultations/planning-for-the-future (last accessed 21 August 2020).

28 See Clay, J., 'How to mend a broken planning system', Cornerstone Development Quarterly – Special Edition (13 August 2020), available at https://cornerstonebarristers.com/news/how-mend-broken-planning-system/ (last accessed 21 August 2020).

29 Ibid.

30 Ibid.

31 Treaty on European Union [2008] OJ C115/13, Art. 5.

32 'Local government funding in England', Institute for Government (10 March 2020), available at https://www.instituteforgovernment.org.uk/explainers/local-government-funding-england (last accessed 20 August 2020).

33 Although this criterion was relaxed slightly by the May government, local tax raising powers remain limited.

34 'Local Government Funding in England'.

35 Cameron, D., Speech to the Conservative Party Conference (2009), available at https://www.theguardian.com/politics/2009/oct/08/david-cameron-speech-in-full (last accessed 20 August 2020); Welfare Reform Act 2012; Universal Credit Regulations 2013.

36 West, A. and Wolfe QC, D., 'Academies, the School System in England and a Vision for the Future', Clare Market Papers No. 23 (LSE, 2018).

37 Academies Act 2010.

38 Levitsky and Ziblatt, *How Democracies Die*.

39 Gebrekidan, S., 'For Autocrats, and Others, Coronavirus is a Chance to

Grab Even More Power', *New York Times* (30 March 2020), available at https://www.nytimes.com/2020/03/30/world/europe/coronavirus-governments-power.html (last accessed 12 November 2020).

40  Dunt, I., 'Coronavirus bill: The biggest expansion in executive power we've seen in our lifetime', Politics.co.uk (18 March 2020), available at https://www.politics.co.uk/blogs/2020/03/18/coronavirus-bill-the-biggest-expansion-in-executive-power-we (last accessed 12 November 2020).

41  Hickman, T., Dixon, E. and Jones, R., 'Coronavirus and Civil Liberties in the UK', *Judicial Review*, 25 (2), 2020, pp. 151–70, available at https://www.ucl.ac.uk/laws/news/2020/apr/dr-tom-hickman-qc-co-authors-report-coronavirus-restrictions-law (last accessed 12 November 2020).

42  Campbell, D., 'Dido Harding: confident, loyal – but with precious little relevant experience', *Guardian* (18 August 2020), available at https://www.theguardian.com/uk-news/2020/aug/18/dido-harding-profile-institute-health-protection (last accessed 20 August 2020); Rodionova, Z., 'TalkTalk given record fine over data breach that led to data theft of nearly 157,000 customers', *Independent* (5 October 2016), available at https://www.independent.co.uk/news/business/news/talktalk-fine-data-breach-theft-customers-information-stolen-record-penalty-a7346316.html (last accessed 20 August 2020).

43  Intelligence and Security Committee, *Russia* (2020), HC 632, §42.

44  Intelligence and Security Committee, *Russia* (2020), HC 632.

45  Sabbagh, D., Harding, L. and Roth, A., 'Russia report reveals UK government failed to investigate Kremlin interference', *Guardian* (21 July 2020), available at https://www.theguardian.com/world/2020/jul/21/russia-report-reveals-uk-government-failed-to-address-kremlin-interference-scottish-referendum-brexit (last accessed 6 November 2020).

46  Ibid.

## Chapter 6: Keeping Secrets

1  For the full story of the Birmingham Pub Bombings and the Birmingham Six see Mullin, C., *Error of Judgment: The True Story of*

the Birmingham Pub Bombings (London: Chatto and Windus, 1986).

2 Ibid.

3 Ibid.

4 Mansfield, M., Memoirs of a Radical Lawyer (London: Bloomsbury, 2010).

5 Coroner for the Birmingham Inquests v Hambleton [2018] EWCA Civ 2081 [2019] 1 W.L.R. 3417.

6 Gupta, T., 'Guildford and Birmingham pub bomb families "need classified IRA file"', BBC (6 February 2020), available at https://www.bbc.co.uk/news/uk-england-51392071 (last accessed 2 November 2020). I make an appearance towards the end of the article . . .

7 De Tocqueville, A., Democracy in America (Indianapolis: Liberty Fund, 2012; first published 1825).

8 Hunt, G., (ed.), The Writings of James Madison, vol. 9 (New York: G.P. Putnam's Sons, 1910).

9 Cobain, The History Thieves.

10 https://democracyweb.org/accountability-principles.

11 Cobain, The History Thieves.

12 Ibid.

13 Ibid.

14 Wintour, P. and Maguire, K., 'The funding scandal that just won't go away', Guardian (20 September 2000), available at https://www.theguardian.com/politics/2000/sep/20/labour.labour1997to99 (last accessed 16 November 2020).

15 Kennedy v Information Commissioner [2015] AC 455 at 153.

16 R (Guardian News Media Ltd) v Westminster Magistrates Court [2013] QB 618 at 1–2.

17 Blair, T., A Journey: My Political Life (London: Random House, 2010), pp. 126–7.

18 Cheung, A., 'We need to know why so many FOI requests are being refused', Institute for Government (22 June 2018), available at https://www.instituteforgovernment.org.uk/blog/we-need-know-why-so-many-foi-requests-are-being-refused (last accessed 21 August 2020).

19 Ibid.

20 Cobain, The History Thieves.

21 Reuters, 'Liz Truss meetings with hard-Brexit group deleted from public register', Guardian (20 August 2020), available at https://

www.theguardian.com/politics/2020/aug/20/liz-truss-meetings-with-hard-brexit-group-deleted-from-public-register (last accessed 16 November 2020).

22 Pegg, D., Lawrence, F. and Evans, R., 'Rightwing thinktank breached charity law by campaigning for a hard Brexit', *Guardian* (5 February 2019), available at https://www.theguardian.com/politics/2019/feb/05/rightwing-thinktank-breached-charity-law-by-campaigning-for-hard-brexit (last accessed 16 November 2020).

23 Independent International Commission on Decommissioning, Report of the IICD (26 September 2005).

24 'The Birmingham Pub Bombings Inquest (1974): Evidence of Chris Mullin', KRW Law (28 March 2019), available at https://krw-law.ie/the-birmingham-pub-bombings-inquest-1974-the-evidence-of-chris-mullin/ (last accessed 16 November 2020).

25 *Metropolitan Police v Information Commissioner* [2008] UKIT EA 2008 0078.

26 *Marriott v Information Commissioner* [2011] UKFTT EA 2010 0183.

27 Duffy, N., 'Tory Vice Chair mocks gender-neutral bathrooms and safe spaces at Labour event', Pink News (6 February 2018), available at https://www.pinknews.co.uk/2018/02/06/tory-vice-chair-mocks-gender-neutral-bathrooms-and-safe-spaces-at-labour-event/ (last accessed 4 November 2020).

28 Mason, R., 'Theresa May criticises university "safe spaces" for shutting down debate', *Guardian* (14 September 2016), available at https://www.theguardian.com/education/2016/sep/14/theresa-may-criticises-university-safe-spaces-for-shutting-down-debate (last accessed 4 November 2020).

29 Hackett, G., 'John Lewis salesman lied his way to £1m job running schools', *The Times* (21 February 2020), available at https://www.thetimes.co.uk/edition/news/john-lewis-salesman-lied-his-way-to-1m-job-running-schools-ptvwlwbgq (last accessed 16 November 2020).

30 *Hackett v Information Commissioner and Secretary of State for Education* [2019] UKFTT 2018_0251 (GRC).

31 This exchange is reproduced from my notes of the hearing which, as they were taken quickly while also conducting cross-examination, were not of the highest quality (I was acting pro bono and did not have the support of a solicitor or junior). I have tried to reproduce

this exchange as accurately as possible and with reference to the Tribunal's written decision in the matter. I am confident that I have preserved the sense of the exchange even if some of the specific language used is not verbatim.

32  *All-Party Parliamentary Group on Extraordinary Rendition v ICO and MoD* [2011] UKUT 153 (AAC) at 57.

33  This is not a verbatim transcript. It is an account of the questioning prepared from my own notes (which were taken while I was conducting the cross-examination) and has been edited for length and clarity.

34  Carr, J., 'DfE spent £50k trying to hide academy chief vetting failure', Schools Week (27 April 2020), available at https://schoolsweek. co.uk/dfe-spent-50k-trying-to-hide-academy-chief-vetting-failure/ (last accessed 16 November 2020).

35  McGovern, Witness Statement.

36  Sample, I., 'Secrecy has harmed the UK government's response to Covid-19 crisis, says top scientist', *Guardian* (2 August 2020), available at https://www.theguardian.com/world/2020/aug/02/secrecy -has-harmed-uk-governments-response-to-covid-19-crisis-says-top-scientist (last accessed 4 November 2020).

37  Sample, I., 'Secrecy has harmed the UK government's response to Covid-19 crisis, says top scientist', *Guardian* (2 August 2020), available at https://www.theguardian.com/world/2020/aug/02/secrecy -has-harmed-uk-governments-response-to-covid-19-crisis-says-top-scientist (last accessed 4 November 2020).

38  Calvert, J., Arbuthnot, G. and Leake, J., 'Coronavirus: 38 days when Britain sleepwalked into disaster', *The Times* (19 April 2020), available at https://www.thetimes.co.uk/article/coronavirus-38-days-when-britain-sleepwalked-into-disaster-hq3b9tlgh (last accessed 4 November 2020).

39  Press, C., 'Coronavirus: The NHS workers wearing bin bags as protection', BBC (5 April 2020), available at https://www.bbc.co.uk /news/health-52145140 (last accessed 15 July 2021).

40  Calvert, Arbuthnot and Leake, 'Coronavirus: 38 days when Britain sleepwalked into disaster'.

41  Sample, I., 'Secrecy has harmed the UK government's response to Covid-19 crisis, says top scientist'.

42  Ibid.

43  Freedman, L., 'Where the science went wrong', *New Statesman* (7

June 2020), available at https://www.newstatesman.com/science-tech/coronavirus/2020/06/where-science-went-wrong (last accessed 4 November 2020).

44 'Coronavirus: "Earlier lockdown would have halved death toll"', BBC (10 June 2020), available at https://www.bbc.co.uk/news/health-52995064 (last accessed 16 November 2020).

45 Morris, A., 'UK government announces plans to end all prosecutions of ex-paramilitaries and former soldiers in Troubles-era cases', *Belfast Telegraph* (14 July 2021), available at https://www.belfasttelegraph.co.uk/news/northern-ireland/uk-government-announces-plans-to-end-all-prosecutions-of-ex-paramilitaries-and-former-soldiers-in-troubles-era-cases-40653455.html (last accessed 23 July 2021).

## Chapter 7: Brits Abroad

1 Joint Committee on Human Rights, *Human Rights Protection in International Agreements* (HC and HL), 2017–19, HC1833, HL310.

2 Constitution Committee, *Parliamentary Scrutiny of Treaties* (HL), 2017–19, 345.

3 Courea, E., 'Boris Johnson heralds "recaptured sovereignty" after Brexit', *Politico* (31 January 2020), available at https://www.politico.eu/article/boris-johnson-heralds-recaptured-sovereignty-after-brexit/ (last accessed 28 August 2020).

4 See Skinner, Q., 'A Genealogy of the Modern State', *Proceedings of the British Academy*, 162, 2009, pp. 325–70, p. 325. The historical accuracy of this term is contested, see Piirimäe, P., 'The Westphalian Myth and the Idea of External Sovereignty', in Kalmo, H. and Skinner, Q., (eds), *Sovereignty in Fragments: The Past, Present, and Future of a Contested Concept* (Cambridge: Cambridge University Press, 2010).

5 Bull, H., *The Anarchical Society: A Study of Order in World Politics* (New York: Columbia University Press, 1995).

6 Madison, J., *The Federalist No. 46* (Belhoff, M., ed.), (New York: Columbia University Press, 1987), p. 239.

7 Ku, J. and Yoo, J., 'Globalization and Sovereignty', Berkeley. *J. Int'l L.* 210, 31, 2013, pp. 210–35.

8 Beitz, C., *The Idea of Human Rights* (Oxford: Oxford University Press, 2009); Ku and Yoo, 'Globalization and Sovereignty'.

9   Constitutional Reform and Government Act 2010, Pt. II.

10  *Montague v (1) The Information Commissioner and (2) The Secretary of State for International Trade*, First Tier Tribunal, General Regulatory Chamber (Information Rights) EA/20190154 at 104.

11  Applebaum, A., *Twilight of Democracy: The Failure of Politics and the parting of Friends* (London: Allen Lane, 2020).

12  Applebaum, *Twilight of Democracy*; García De Blas, E., 'Echoes of Franco as Spain's far right tells PM his government is "worst in 80 years"', *El País* (10 September 2020), available at https://english.elpais.com/politics/2020-09-10/echoes-of-franco-as-spains-far-right-tells-pm-his-government-is-worst-in-80-years.html (last accessed 17 November 2020).

13  Applebaum, *Twilight of Democracy*.

14  Woodcock, A., 'Government sees off Tory rebellion to defeat "genocide amendment"', *Independent* (22 March 2021), available at https://www.independent.co.uk/news/uk/politics/china-xinjiang-genocide-trade-bill-b1820812.html (last accessed 15 July 2021).

15  See Fowles, S., 'FPC Briefing: How Investment Treaties have a chilling effect on Human Rights', Foreign Policy Centre (11 May 2017), available at https://fpc.org.uk/fpc-briefing-how-investment-treaties-have-a-chilling-effect-on-human-rights/ (last accessed 31 August 2020).

16  Tienhaara, K., 'Investor State Dispute Settlement', in Drahos, P., (ed.), *Regulatory Theory* (Canberra: ANU Press, 2017), p. 681; Fowles, 'How Investment Treaties have a chilling effect on Human Rights'; *Compañia del Desarrollo de Santa Elena S.A. v. Republic of Costa Rica*, 39 ILM 317 (2000); *Metalclad Corporation v. The United Mexican States*, ICSID Case No. ARB(AF)/97/1; Thakur, T., 'Reforming the investor-state dispute settlement mechanism and the host state's right to regulate: a critical assessment', (2020) 6 I.J.I.L.; *Ethyl v Canada* 78 International Legal Materials (1999), pp. 708–31; Tienhaara, K., 'Regulatory Chill in a Warming World: The Threat to Climate Policy Posed by Investor-State Dispute Settlement', (2018) 7 T.E.L. 2, p. 234.

17  Anghie, A., *Imperialism, Sovereignty and the Making of International Law* (Cambridge: Cambridge University Press, 2007).

18  Ku and Yoo, 'Globalization and Sovereignty'.

19  O'Carroll, L., 'Brexit "teething problems" endemic and could ruin us,

say UK businesses', *Guardian* (31 January 2021), available at https://www.theguardian.com/politics/2021/jan/31/brexit-trade-troubles-teething-problems-endemic-disruption (last accessed 15 July 2021).

20 Toynbee, P., 'The Brexit deal was astonishingly bad, and every day the evidence piles up', *Guardian* (16 March 2021), available at https://www.theguardian.com/commentisfree/2021/mar/16/brexit-deal-bad-evidence-trade (last accessed 15 July 2021).

## Chapter 8: Media Barons, Old and New

1 Younge, G., 'The Tories can't win without the press. This isn't how democracy works', *Guardian* (15 November 2019).

2 Runciman, *How Democracy Ends*; Levitsky and Ziblatt, *How Democracies Die*.

3 *R (Liberal Democrats and Scottish National Party) v ITV* [2019] EWHC 3282 (Admin), Per Coppel QC and Fowles.

4 See, for example, Democratic Audit, 'Democratic Audit 2018: The UK's Changing Democracy', (2018).

5 Williams, C., *Max Beaverbrook: Not Quite a Gentleman* (London: Biteback Publishing, 2019).

6 Thompson, J. L., *Northcliffe: Press Baron in Politics, 1865–1922* (London: John Murray, 2000).

7 Standing, G., *The Corruption of Capitalism* (London: Biteback Publishing, 2021).

8 Ibid.

9 Geoghegan, P., *Democracy for Sale* (London: Head of Zeus, 2020).

10 https://en.wikipedia.org/wiki/Richard_Desmond#Express_Newspapers

11 Porter, C., 'The Rise of Evgeny Lebedev', *New York Times* (31 December 2014), available at https://www.nytimes.com/2015/01/01/style/the-rise-of-evgeny-lebedev.html (last accessed 23 November 2020).

12 Woodcock, A., 'The Independent's Evgeny Lebedev awarded peerage by PM', *Independent* (31 July 2020), available at https://www.independent.co.uk/news/uk/politics/evgeny-lebedev-lord-peerage-boris-johnson-a9648701.html (last accessed 23 November 2020).

13 See, National Readership Survey, available at http://www.nrs.co.uk (last accessed 23 November 2020); and Jones, E., 'Five reasons we don't have a free and independent press in the UK and what we can do about it', Open Democracy (18 April 2019). The figures in the survey cited here may seem slightly high (given that the total population of the UK is not much more than 66 million). This is because the surveys record the readership of each paper, meaning that they include individuals who read more than one newspaper.

14 Shipman, T., *All Out War: The Full Story of How Brexit Sank Britain's Political Class* (London: William Collins, 2016).

15 Geoghegan, P., *Democracy for Sale: Dark Money and Dirty Politics* (London: Apollo, 2020).

16 Standing, *The Corruption of Capitalism*.

17 Ladd, J. M. and Lenz, G., 'Exploiting a Rare Communication Shift to Document the Persuasive Power of the News Media', *American Journal of Political Science*, 53 (2), 2009, pp. 394–410.

18 Naughton, J., 'Reports of social media's influence on voters are exaggerated', *Guardian* (15 February 2020).

19 'Leveson Inquiry: Matt Hancock axes proposed second stage', BBC (1 March 2018), available at https://www.bbc.co.uk/news/uk-politics-43240230 (last accessed 23 November 2020).

20 Sweney, M., 'The rise of LBC's owner Global and how it is now poaching BBC stars', *Guardian* (24 February 2022), available at: https://www.theguardian.com/media/2022/feb/24/the-rise-of-lbcs-owner-global-and-how-it-is-now-poaching-bbc-stars (last accessed 23 March 2022).

21 Waterson, J., 'Rupert Murdoch's talkRadio argued it had very few listeners to avoid fine', *Guardian* (17 February 2020), available at: https://www.theguardian.com/media/2020/feb/17/rupert-murdoch-talkradio-argued-it-had-very-few-listeners-to-avoid-fine (last accessed 23 March 2022).

22 Volpicelli, G. M., 'Can a British Fox News work?', *Wired* (4 September 2020), available at https://www.wired.co.uk/article/british-fox-news (last accessed 23 November 2020).

23 Duffy, N., 'Tory MPs demand Boris Johnson take action after BBC censors "f****t" from Fairytale of New York', Pink News (23 November 2020), available at https://www.pinknews.co.uk/2020/

11/23/tory-mps-bbc-license-fee-fairytale-new-york-common-sense
/ (last accessed 23 November 2020).

24  Gardner, B., 'Exclusive: BBC's new boss threatens to axe Left-wing comedy shows', *Telegraph* (31 August 2020), available at https://www.telegraph.co.uk/news/2020/08/31/exclusive-bbcs-new-boss-threatens-axe-left-wing-comedy-shows/ (last accessed 23 November 2020).

25  Wahl-Jorgensen, K., et al., 'BBC Breadth of Opinion Review' (University of Cardiff, 2013).

26  Berry, M., 'How Biased is the BBC?', The Conversation (23 August 2013).

27  Gaber, I., 'When you actually look into it, the BBC has a centre-right bias – which explains its coverage of Corbyn', *Independent* (18 July 2017), available at https://www.independent.co.uk/voices/bbc-bias-jeremy-corbyn-labour-centre-right-robbie-gibb-theresa-may-laura-keunssberg-andrew-marr-a7844826.html (last accessed 23 November 2020).

28  Robertson, J., 'BBC bias and the Scots referendum – new report', Open Democracy (21 February 2014).

29  Berry, 'How Biased is the BBC?'.

30  Gaber, I., 'When you actually look into it, the BBC has a centre-right bias'.

31  'The Overton Window', Mackinac Center for Public Policy (2019), available at https://www.mackinac.org/OvertonWindow (last accessed 23 November 2020).

32  Hughes, C., 'It's Time to Break Up Facebook', *New York Times* (9 May 2019), available at https://www.nytimes.com/2019/05/09/opinion/sunday/chris-hughes-facebook-zuckerberg.html (last accessed 23 November 2020).

33  Rushe, D., 'Twitter and activist investor agree on truce to keep Jack Dorsey as chief', *Guardian* (9 March 2020), available at https://www.theguardian.com/business/2020/mar/09/twitter-jack-dorsey-elliott-management-agreement (last accessed 23 November 2020).

34  Howard, P. N., *Lie Machines: How to save democracy from Troll Armies, Deceitful Robots, Junk News, Operations and Political Operatives* (New Haven: Yale University Press, 2020).

35  While it is sometimes possible to track the owner of an anonymous account, it takes relatively little technical expertise to ensure that one is all but untraceable. Howard, *Lie Machines*.

36  Howard, *Lie Machines*.
37  United States and Schiff, R. (2019), 'Russian Active Measures and Interference in the 2016 US Election', 116th Congress, Senate Report 116-XX; Howard, *Lie Machines*.
38  Intelligence and Security Committee, *Russia* (2020), HC 632.
39  Geoghegan, *Democracy for Sale*; Howard, *Lie Machines*.

## Chapter 9: Populism: Weaponised Bullshit

1  Eatwell, R. and Goodwin, M., *National Populism: The Revolt Against Liberal Democracy* (London: Pelican, 2018).
2  Ashcroft, Lord, 'How the United Kingdom voted on Thursday . . . and why', Lord Ashcroft Polls (24 June 2016), available at http://lordashcroftpolls.com/2016/06/how-the-united-kingdom-voted-and-why/; Kaufmann, E., 'It's NOT the economy, stupid: Brexit as a story of personal values', LSE (7 July 2016), available at http://blogs.lse.ac.uk/politicsandpolicy/personal-values-brexit-vote/.
3  Stocker, *English Uprising*.
4  Wootton, D., Twitter (13 November 2020), available at https://twitter.com/danwootton/status/1327300783545741312 (last accessed 14 November 2020).
5  Geoghan, *Democracy for Sale*.
6  Cadwalladr, C., 'Vote Leave donations: the dark ads, the mystery "letter" – and Brexit's online guru', *Observer* (25 November 2017), available at https://www.theguardian.com/politics/2017/nov/25/vote-leave-dominic-cummings-online-guru-mystery-letter-dark-ads (last accessed 14 November 2020).
7  Swinford, S., Wright, O. and Coles, O., 'Dominic Cummings forced out in purge of Brexiteers', *The Times* (14 November 2020), available at https://www.thetimes.co.uk/article/dominic-cummings-forced-out-in-purge-of-brexiteers-5tg2cmgqr (last accessed 14 November 2020).
8  Geoghan, *Democracy for Sale*.
9  Standing, G., *A Precariat Charter: From Denizens to Citizens* (London: Bloomsbury, 2014).
10  Standing G., *The Precariat*, (London: Bloomsbury, 2011).
11  Butler, P., 'Welfare spending for UK's poorest shrinks by £37bn',

*Guardian* (23 September 2018), available at https://www.theguardian.com/politics/2018/sep/23/welfare-spending-uk-poorest-austerity-frank-field (last accessed 27 March 2021).

12  Butler, P., 'Cost of rolling out universal credit rises by £1.4bn, say auditors', *Guardian* (10 July 2020), available at https://www.theguardian.com/society/2020/jul/10/cost-of-rolling-out-universal-credit-rises-by-14bn-say-auditors (last accessed 27 March 2021).

13  Owen, G., 'EXPOSED: How Labour depends on the votes of Welfare Britain', Mail Online (10 November 2009), available at https://www.dailymail.co.uk/news/article-1226031/EXPOSED-How-Labour-depends-votes-Welfare-Britain.html (last accessed 19 August 2020).

14  Lawrence, F., McIntyre, N. and Butler, P., 'Labour councils in England hit harder by austerity than Tory areas', *Guardian* (21 June 2020), available at https://www.theguardian.com/business/2020/jun/21/exclusive-labour-councils-in-england-hit-harder-by-austerity-than-tory-areas (last accessed 14 August 2020).

15  Milne, S., *The Enemy Within: The Secret War Against the Miners* (London: Verso, 2004).

16  This was achieved by requiring a minimum turnout of 50% in all strike ballots. No such minimum turnouts are imposed on any other part of our democracy even when the votes will have far greater impact than a strike. Politicians resisted, for example, a requirement for a minimum turnout in the Brexit referendum and MPs can be elected on a turnout of a single person.

17  By limiting the amount of money they can spend in an election year.

18  Geoghegan, *Democracy for Sale*.

19  'Wages and salaries annual growth rate %', Office for National Statistics (23 December 2016), available at https://www.ons.gov.uk/economy/grossdomesticproductgdp/timeseries/kgq2/qna (last accessed 16 July 2021).

20  'UK average monthly property rent soars to highest on record', Martin & Co (23 August 2011), available at https://www.martinco.com/estate-agents-and-letting-agents/branch/camden/news/uk-average-monthly-property-rent-soars-to-highest-on-record-2526 (last accessed 16 July 2021).

21  Butler, P. and Booth, R., 'Key Points from UN envoy's report on poverty in Britain', *Guardian* (16 November 2018).

22   Bulman, M., 'Food Bank use in UK reaches highest rate on record as benefits fail to cover basic costs', *Independent* (24 April 2018).

23   Standing, *A Precariat Charter*.

24   Garside, J., 'Recession rich: Britain's wealthiest double net worth since crisis', *Guardian* (26 April 2015).

25   Schmuecker, K., 'Tuesday's Spring Statement is an opportunity to right the wrong of in-work poverty', Joseph Rowntree Foundation (12 March 2018).

26   'Universal Credit and Food Banks', The Trussell Trust (2019), available at https://www.trusselltrust.org/what-we-do/research-advocacy/universal-credit-and-foodbank-use/; Fitzpatrick, S., et al., 'The homelessness monitor: England 2018', Crisis (2018); Butler, P., 'New study finds 4.5 million UK children living in poverty', *Guardian* (16 September 2018); Bulman, M. (2018) 'Child Homelessness in England Rises to Highest Level in 12 Years, New Figures Show', *Independent* (13 December 2018); 'Homeless Die 30 Years Younger than Average', NHS (21 December 2011).

27   Standing, *The Corruption of Capitalism*.

28   Ibid.

29   See *Cowan v Scargill* [1985] Ch. 270.

30   Herrera, G. L., Morelli, H. and Sonno, M., 'Demand and Supply Populism', unpublished manuscript, Einaudi Institute, Warwick University, Bocconi University and Catholic University of Leuven (2017).

31   Eichengreen, B., *The Populist Temptation: Economic Grievance and Political Reaction in the Modern Era* (New York: Oxford University Press, 2018); Nunn, N., Qian, N. and Wen, J., 'Trust, Growth, and Political Stability', unpublished manuscript, Harvard University (2016).

32   'Issues Index: Trends 1988–1997', Ipsos MORI (1 May 1997), available at https://www.ipsos.com/ipsos-mori/en-uk/issues-index-trends-1988-1997 (last accessed 4 January 2022).

33   Stocker, *English Uprising*.

34   'Issues Index: 2007 onwards', Ipsos MORI (24 March 2014), available at https://www.ipsos.com/ipsos-mori/en-uk/issues-index-2007-onwards , available at https://www.ipsos.com/ipsos-mori/en-uk/issues-index-2007-onwards (last accessed 4 January 2022).

35   Eichengreen, *The Populist Temptation*.

36   'The Fiscal Impact of Immigration on the UK', Oxford Economics

(2018), available at https://www.oxfordeconomics.com/recent-releases/8747673d-3b26-439b-9693-0e250df6dbba (last accessed 21 September 2020); Eichengreen, *The Populist Temptation*.

37  Eichengreen, *The Populist Temptation*.

38  Applebaum, *Twilight of Democracy*.

39  Eichengreen, *The Populist Temptation*.

## Chapter 10: Crushing Dissent

1  *Leigh v Commissioner of Police for the Metropolis* [2021] EWHC 661 (Admin).

2  Quoted in *Hubbard v Pitt* [1976] QB 142 (CA) at 174.

3  *Hubbard v Pitt* [1976] QB 142 (CA).

4  See *Handyside v UK* (5493/72) [1976] ECHR 5 at 49; *Saska v Hungary* 58050/08 – HEJUD [2012] ECHR 1981 at 21–3; *Sunday Times v UK* (1979) 2 EHRR 245.

5  All-Party Parliamentary Group on Democracy and the Constitution, *Police Power and the Right to Peaceful Protest* (HC/HL 2019–21), p. 82.

6  All-Party Parliamentary Group on Democracy and the Constitution, *Police Power and the Right to Peaceful Protest* (HC/HL 2019–21), pp. 28–9.

7  All-Party Parliamentary Group on Democracy and the Constitution, *Police Power and the Right to Peaceful Protest* (HC/HL 2019–21), pp. 29–30.

8  *Kudrivicius v Lithuania* [2013] ECHR 1310 at 159–60.

9  All-Party Parliamentary Group on Democracy and the Constitution, *Police Power and the Right to Peaceful Protest* (HC/HL 2019–21), p. 41.

10  HMIC, 'Adapting to protest: nurturing the British model of policing' (2009).

11  HMIC, 'Getting the balance right' (2020); Gilmore, J., et al., 'Policing the UK's anti-fracking movement: facilitating peaceful protest of facilitating the industry?' *Peace Human Rights Governance*, 4 (3), 2020, pp. 349–90.

12  'Spycops Targets: a Who's Who', Undercover Research Group, available at http://undercoverresearch.net/spycops-targets-a-whos-who/ (last accessed 20 July 2021).

13 Parveen, N., 'Priti Patel describes Black Lives Matter protests as "dreadful"', *Guardian* (12 February 2021), available at https://www.theguardian.com/politics/2021/feb/12/priti-patel-hits-out-at-dreadful-black-lives-matters-protests (last accessed 4 January 2022).

14 Trilling, 'Why is the UK government suddenly targeting "critical race theory"'; Adams, G. K., 'Museum of the Home to "reflect further" on Geffrye statue', Museums Association (8 September 2020), available at https://www.museumsassociation.org/museums-journal/news/2020/09/museum-of-the-home-to-reflect-further-on-fate-of-geffrye-statue/ (last accessed 18 November 2020); Stubley, 'Museums risk funding cuts if they remove controversial objects, culture secretary warns'; Hope, C., 'National Trust's slavery review was "unfortunate" and charity "should go back to core functions"', *Telegraph* (11 November 2020), available at https://www.telegraph.co.uk/news/2020/11/11/national-trusts-slavery-review-unfortunate-charity-should-go/ (last accessed 18 November 2020).

15 Gilmore, et al., 'Policing the UK's Anti-fracking Movement'.

16 Dodd, V., Mohdin, A. and Allegretti, A., 'Cressida Dick refuses to quit over vigil policing and dismisses "armchair critics"', *Guardian* (15 March 2021), available at https://www.theguardian.com/uk-news/2021/mar/14/london-mayor-sadiq-khan-rebukes-met-chief-cressida-dick-policing-sarah-everard-vigil (last accessed 20 July 2021).

17 Dodd, V., 'De Menezes family call for Cressida Dick to be barred from leading Met', *Guardian* (17 February 2017), available at https://www.theguardian.com/uk-news/2017/feb/17/de-menezes-family-call-cressida-dick-barred-from-leading-met (last accessed 20 July 2021).

18 Walker, A., and Blackall, M., 'Why did Cressida Dick resign? The failings which left the Met Police Commissioner "no choice" but to quit', *i* (11 February 2022), available at: https://inews.co.uk/news/cressida-dick-resign-why-met-police-commissioner-quit-failings-explained-1455269 (last accessed 24 March 2022).

19 All-Party Parliamentary Group on Democracy and the Constitution, *Police Power and the Right to Peaceful Protest* (HC/HL 2019–21), p. 69.

20  HMICFRS, 'The Sarah Everard Vigil' (2021), p. 47.

21  All-Party Parliamentary Group on Democracy and the Constitution, *Police Power and the Right to Peaceful Protest*, p. 42.

22  Dodd, V., 'Police watchdog accused of skewing report to back protests clampdown', *Guardian* (31 March 2021), available at https://www. theguardian.com/uk-news/2021/mar/31/police-watchdog-accused-of-skewing-report-to-back-protests-clampdown (last accessed 20 July 2021).

23  Zhao, Y., *Who's Afraid of the Big Bad Dragon: Why China has the best (and worst) education system in the world* (New York: Jossey-Bass, 2014).

24  Young, M. and Dube, L., 'State of the Unions: How to restore free association and expression, combat extremism and make student unions effective', Adam Smith Institute (20 September 2020).

25  'The state of the (student) unions', Adam Smith Institute.

26  Bakare, L., '"Triple whammy" of funding cuts has left UK arts vulnerable – report', *Guardian* (8 June 2020), available at https://www. theguardian.com/culture/2020/jun/08/triple-whammy-of-funding -cuts-has-left-uk-arts-vulnerable-report (last accessed 18 November 2020).

27  Ibid.

28  Busby, E., 'Council funds for libraries, museums and galleries cut by nearly £400m over eight years, figures reveal', *Independent* (25 January 2019), available at https://www.independent.co.uk/news/uk/home -news/libraries-museums-arts-galleries-funding-recourses-county-council-network-cnn-social-care-a8741271.html (last accessed 22 October 2020).

29  Serota, N., 'More funding for the arts could benefit everyone in the country', *Evening Standard* (17 November 2017), available at https:/ /www.standard.co.uk/comment/comment/more-funding-for-the-arts-could-benefit-everyone-in-the-country-a3694116.html    (last accessed 22 October 2020).

30  CEBR, 'Contribution of the arts and culture industry to the UK economy', Arts Council England (April 2019), available at https:// www.artscouncil.org.uk/sites/default/files/download-file/ Economic%20impact%20of%20arts%20and%20culture%20on%20 the%20national%20economy%20FINAL_0_0.PDF (last accessed 22 October 2020).

31  Busby, 'Council funds for libraries, museums, and galleries cut by nearly £400m over eight years, figures reveal'.

32  Unlock Democracy, Written evidence to the House of Commons Political and Constitutional Reform Committee (August 2013), available at https://publications.parliament.uk/pa/cm201314/cmselect/cmpolcon/601/601vw13.htm (last accessed 16 October 2020).

33  Cusick, J., 'Exclusive: David Cameron condemned over "ridiculous" reforms to lobbying', *Independent* (20 August 2013), available at https://www.independent.co.uk/news/uk/politics/exclusive-david -cameron-condemned-over-ridiculous-reforms-lobbying-8773473. html (last accessed 16 October 2020).

34  Wintour, P., 'Labour funding will be hit hard by changes to political levy system', *Guardian* (27 May 2015), available at https://www.theguardian.com/politics/2015/may/27/labour-funding-hit-change-political-levy-bill  (last  accessed  18 November 2020).

## Conclusion: Revitalising the Constitution

1  Hardman, *Why We Get the Wrong Politicians*.

2  Feldman, D., 'The Politics and People of Entick v Carrington', in Tompkins, A. and Scott., P., *Entick v Carrington: 250 Years of the Rule of Law* (Oxford: Hart, 2015).

3  Hardman, *Why We Get the Wrong Politicians*.

4  Ibid.

5  See CPR 32 and Ormerod, D., et al., *Blackstone's Criminal Practice* (London: Oxford University Press, 2019), s. F4.

6  Constitutional Reform Act 2005, s. 17; Promissory Oaths Act 1868, s. 6A.

7  As set out in detail by Lord Hope in *West v Secretary of State for Scotland* 1992 SC 385 at 412.

8  *Wightman and others v Secretary of State for Exiting the European Union (No. 2)* [2018] CSIH 62, 2019 SC 111 at 67.

9  UK Government, 'Budget 2020' (12 March 2020), available at https://www.gov.uk/government/publications/budget-2020-documents/budget-2020 (last accessed 17 June 2020).

10  Neate, R., 'Feeble oversight of UK's Covid Loan schemes was a gift to fraudsters', *Guardian* (25 January 2022), Available at: https://www.theguardian.com/business/2022/jan/25/feeble-oversight-of-uks-covid-loan-schemes-was-a-gift-to-fraudsters (last accessed 24 March 2022).

DR SAM FOWLES is a barrister specialising in public and constitutional law, with experience in the UK, US, Australia and at the Council of Europe. He has worked on several of the most significant political cases of recent years and is the director of the Institute for Constitutional and Democratic Research. He regularly writes for politics.co.uk.